To

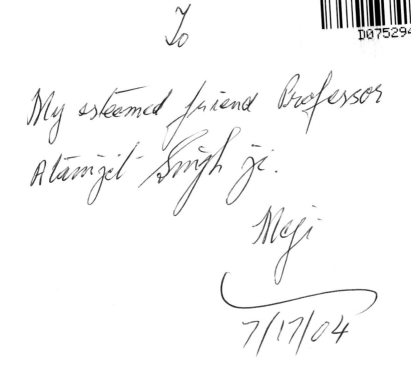

My esteemed friend Professor
Alamjit Singh ji.

Myi

7/17/04

A Sikh's Paradigm For Universal Peace

Meji Singh, Ph.D., Gyani

Foreword by Ernest F. Pecci, MD

Preface by Rev. Paul Chaffee

The Cover of the book is designed by Jani Beckwith, reflecting the following symbols:

Nishan Sahib has a chakra (circle) flanked by two swords and a two-edged dagger (khanda) in the middle. The chakra signifies the Infinite Divine. The swords and the khanda signify the Supreme Power.

Ik Onkar means there is one Creator who manifests Itself in Its Creation. Jani integrated both in the left hand corner of the cover.

The Indus Valley: The five rivers of Punjab are the tributaries of the Indus river, creating the Indus Valley.

A Sikh's Paradigm For Universal Peace

Meji Singh, PhD, Gyani

Library of Congress Cataloging-in-Publication Data

Singh, Meji.
   A Sikh's paradigm for universal peace / Meji Singh.
      p. cm.
   Includes bibliographical references.
   ISBN 1-929331-08-8
   1. Religious life--Sikhism. 2. Sikhism--Doctrines. 3.
Sikhism--History. 4. Peace--Religious aspects--Sikhism.
I. Title.

   BL2018.37.S475 2004
   294.6'44--dc22
                                        2004006739

A Sikh's Paradigm For Universal Peace

A Tribute To
Sri Guru Gobind Singh Ji: The Khalsa

Meji Singh, PhD, Gyani

PAVIOR

2810 Camino Diablo, #10 • Walnut Creek, CA 94596

Mankind's Religious future may be obscure; yet one thing can be foreseen. The living higher religions are going to influence each other more than ever before in the days of increasing communication between all parts of the world and all branches of the human race. In this coming religious debate, the Sikh religion, and its scriptures, the *Adi Granth*, will have something of special value to say to the rest of the world.

-Arnold Toynbee

The Loving Spirit

Simi Singh

The Creator is a spirit in every one of us.
 It does not please Creator just to make a fuss.

Clothing or your customs make no difference to
The Kind and Loving spirit that created me and you.

I am thankful to the Spirit for all I have in Life,
Though with the joy I have had my share of trouble and strife.

Feel the joy of living, take a look at what you've got.
It all is very precious even if it's not a lot.

When life gets you down and no one understands
The loving Spirit reaches out with in-vi-sible hands!

My daughter, Simi was thirteen years old when she wrote this poem.

Dedicated

To

The Memory of My Sisters

Jaswant Kaur Bhen ji
Rattan Kaur Bhen ji
And My Cousin Janak

They never gave a lecture on Sikhi,
but we could experience it in their loving presence.

Acknowledgments

April 13, 1999 marked the 300th anniversary of the birth of the Khalsa (The Pure One). Since I was born a Sikh, I tried to review my understanding of the Sikh spiritual practice and how it culminated into the creation of Sant Sipahi (Spiritual Warrior) army of the Khalsa. I wondered about the implications of this practice for my own life and the world around me. As a tribute to Sri Guru Gobind Singh ji, the creator of Khalsa, I completed the manuscript by the Baisakhi Festival of April 1999. I sent the manuscript to 34 friends of different age groups, religions, and professions throughout the world. I also sent them a Feedback Questionnaire (Appendix I). The following friends gave me extensive feedback that has helped me in my own understanding of different spiritual practices and the underlying unity of all faiths. I am deeply indebted to all of them.

1. Surinder Singh Arora, M.D. Ottawa, Canada
2. Rupinder Kaur Arora, M.D. Ottawa, Canada
3. Kusum Bhat, Ph.D. Psychologist, Pleasant Hill, California
4. Surinder S. Bajwa, Engineer, Pleasant Hill, California
5. Greg Bogart, Ph.D., Transpersonal Psychologist, El Cerrito, California
6. H.S. Dilgir, Retired Professor of Journalism, Punjab University, India
7. Vajid Jafri, Engineer and Entrepreneur, Redwood City, California
8. Mary Ellen Donald, M.S.W., Middle Eastern Percussionist, Oakland
9. Jani Beckwith, M.A. Artist, Buddhist Practitioner, Vallejo, CA
10. Brother Ralph Femandes, Franciscan Order, Ottawa, Canada
11. Sat Santokh Singh Khalsa, Sikh Dharma, San Leandro, CA
12. Jaspreet K. Khangura, High School Student, Walnut Creek, CA
13. Harmesh Kumar, Ph.D. Neuro-psychologist, Concord, CA
14. Sheik Mehmet Selim Ozic, Sufi Master, Istanbul, Turkey

15. Amarjit K. Pannu, Biochemist and Punjabi Writer, Pinole, CA
16. Kimpreet K. Puar, B.A., Oakland CA
17. Khalil Rahmany, Ph.D. Psychologist, Islamic Scholar, Concord, CA
18. G.S. Sachdev, Master of Bamboo Flute, San Rafael, CA
19. Joty Sikand, Psy.D, Director of Preventive Services, The Hume Center, Concord, CA
20. Gurnam Singh Sidhu-Brar, Ph.D., Nuclear Physicist, Oakland, CA
21. Satinder Pal Singh, Ph.D., Architect, Oakland, CA
22. Daleep K. Tiwana, Ph.D., Novelist and Professor, Punjabi University, Patiala, Punjab, India
23. Jodh Singh, Ph.D. Professor of Sikhism, Punjabi University, Punjab, India
24. Juve Vela, Psy.D.Clinical Psychology, Berkeley, California
25. Diane Whiting, M.F.C.C., Counselor, Idaho
26. Romesh and Asha Seth, Producers, Golden Temple Documentary

I am grateful to Dr. Joginder S. Ahluwalia for reviewing and correcting all the Gurbani quotes and the Roman spellings of Punjabi quotes. He has made a major contribution to the final draft of the book. I have learnt a lot from him

Rev. Paul Chaffee made the book reader friendly by pointing out the unclarity of statements and words for the Western readers and the Sikh children born in the West.

I would appreciate it if the reader would fill out the Feedback Question-naire and send it to me with his/her comments. I am also thankful to Jani Beckwith for designing the cover and to Iqbal S. Khalsa of the California Copy Source for filling in the colors on the cover, making corrections on several revisions of the draft and completing the design of the book.

Table of Contents

I
PREFACE

A Sikh's Paradigm for Universal Peace is a treasury of Sikh scripture, history, and stories. The treasury has been assembled and shaped by R. K. Janmeja Singh, known as Meji to family, friends, and students. Meji has one foot in the Indus Valley, where he was born and raised and where Sikhism had its beginning 500 years ago; the other in northern California's Bay Area, where he looks back on half a century of teaching and practicing community psychiatry as a visionary psychologist. Meji the teacher, is particularly known for his engaged listening, a rare gift that creates a learning context which promotes a student's self-discovery.

Meji's book opens us to his rich spiritual, religious heritage — a tradition, sad to say, known in the West primarily through the turbans worn by many Sikh men. Most Americans, including some with Sikh parents, do not know that Sikhism is a religion of the heart, that its founder was a poet-singer and its scripture comes in the form of devotional hymns, that it is one of the world's most interfaith-friendly religions, or that Sikhs have an ancient, still vital reputation for acting intuitively and immediately to help whenever they find someone in crisis.

This book is not the introductory primer on Sikhism, one of the world's youngest major religions, you might find in an encyclopedia, library, or bookstore. Instead, Meji personally surveys a universe conveyed through devotional poetry, a dramatic, often poignant historical record, and robust ethical grounding. His text weaves its way through Sikh theological assumptions, generous quotations from Sikh scripture, a many-layered history, and dozens of stories that bring the narrative to life.

Underlying everything else is an explication of Haumain, ego-driven consciousness, and Naam, or divine cosmic consciousness, both of them appropriate elements in our lives. But when the former succumbs to attachment, pride, and pain, the latter can be an ultimate source of peace and harmony. Without being moralistic, the comparison gives Sikhism's mystical conception of reality an ethical grounding for our daily lives.

This is a passionate book because Meji Singh cares so passionately about people, about individuals whose lives, encumbered by the ways of the world, can be empowered with a peace and harmony that transcends explanations and our differences.

Rev. Paul Chaffee
Executive Director
Interfaith Center at the Presidio
San Francisco

II
FOREWORD

I first met Dr. Meji Singh more than 35 years ago when I attended the Center for Training in Community Psychiatry in Berkeley, California. We shared common interests in psychology and spirituality, and immediately became good friends.

In 1968, Meji designed a beautiful one-story home in the Berkeley hills in the shape of a large square that enclosed a central garden area. He set aside one of the rooms surrounding this garden for his daily meditation practice (*Gurdwara*). I was so impressed with the energy I felt when I was invited into this room, that I decided to set aside a special place in my own home for meditation. This proved to be the greatest gift he could have given to me.

This book's philosophy is consistent with the great spiritual teachers from many different cultures: that we are all on a spiritual journey to find our way home to the Source who created us. What makes this book so powerful for the reader; Meji speaks as one who lives his philosophy.

This physical world has been called "The Veil of Tears." Few can say that they have not experienced grief while alive. Yet, our greatest grief, which the mind has blocked out, is the grief of separation from our Creator. The Creator in every generation and culture sends aspects of Himself in the form of prophets, avatars, teachers and gurus who teach us to turn away from our false identity and our preoccupation with mortal things, and return to the eternal joy of Oneness. All major religions are consistent with this teaching, that God sends God-enlightened beings to lead us out of the darkness of ignorance.

Words spoken by a guru have great power to awaken us to the power within ourselves. Meditating on the presence of the guru, or chanting the words spoken by a guru take on His power that is shared by the repetition of the words. But this must be done with a deep sense of homage, not with idle or mechanical repetition that would keep them from reaching the heart. Through prayer, meditation, chanting and devotional love to the presence of the memory of an enlightened saint or guru, we might slowly fill our inner loneliness with our true and divine nature.

This book is a great gift to the Westerner who is interested in inter-faith understanding. It is a particularly important offering to Sikh parents, children and youth who live outside of Punjab and can understand the importance of Sikh spiritual practice and its relevance to their life and the realities around them.

In order to fully appreciate this book by Meji, the teachings must not only be read, they must be breathed and practiced.

> Ernest F. Pecci, MD
> Founding President
> Rosebridge Graduate School of Integrative Psychology
> (was bought by American School of Professional Psychology,
> now Argosy University)
> Richmond, California

III
INTRODUCTION

It may be a quiet whisper, or it may resonate throughout our body and mind; all of us are on a spiritual journey whether or not we are aware of it. We come from the same Creative Source into this physical world to experience it, learn from it, not to make value judgments, and then to return to the Source. At physical birth, we become separated and begin to develop our separate "I" (Haumain)[1] consciousness, which helps us to experience this world in our unique way, according to our given form and our role in life:

> *jit jit laia tit tit Lagana*
> *na ko moor nahin ko siana*

Where ever one is placed there one serves.
There is no fool or a wise person
- Guru Arjan Dev ji, SGGS[2] - P. 914

> *aval allah noor upaia, kudrat ke sabh bande*
> *ek noor te sabh jag upjia, kaun bhale kaun munde.*

First, Allah created Light
All humans are Nature's creation
All creation emanates from the same Light
Then who are good and who are bad?
- Bhagat Kabir ji, SGGS - P. 1349

Making punitive value judgments on each other is to criticize the Creator. It is possible to awaken the Divine Creator consciousness and be one with

---

[1] Haumain literally means, "I am". It is a consciousness that I am the doer and I am the cause. The Divine created this consciousness to experience Itself in different forms. Attachment to Haumain and forgetting the Source is the cause of all suffering.
[2] SGGS - Sri Guru Granth Sahib

the Divine while we are still alive. The Divine has fully revealed Itself in human form from time to time and presented us with a model for our own transformation.

har jug jug bhagat upaia
paij rakhda aya ram raje

Har (Divine) manifested Itself in devotees throughout ages
And protected their honor, Ram (Divine) ordained it so.
- Guru Ramdas ji, SGGS - P. 451

The above reference to "protected their honor" means the Divine helped Its devotees to live in Its consciousness, in spite of the temptations or fear created by the Haumain based world. Christ[3] was crucified but did not stray from his spiritual path. There are numerous such manifestations both known and unknown, such as Prahalad, Namdev, Guru Nanak - Guru Gobind Singh, Moses, Hazarat Muhammad Sahib, Budha, Krishna and so on and so on. These spiritual beings provided us with a model of living in a spiritual consciousness. They appeared throughout human history and across continents.

The tragedy is that quite often the enlightened being is taken over by those who live in Haumain consciousness and are confined to religious walls; the spirit is suffocated in the sectarian squeeze. Religion is usually initiated with good intentions. Soon, the religion is taken over by organizational processes, becomes a tool to control others, and is used for worldly glory, achievements and vested sectarian interests. It is pointless to condemn or make punitive value judgments on religious practices, which are usually contrary to the spiritual vision. Nevertheless religious practices do serve some purpose. For instance, I would never have been introduced to Gurbani[4] if my family had not taken me to the Gurdwaras[5]. Currently, people are beginning to wake up to their spiritual inheritance.

Religious leaders are becoming more vocal about practicing "Love," the essence of all religions. They raise their voices against injustice and war, support human rights, and work toward the preservation of this planet as the beautiful creation of our Creator.

For example, the President of the Council of Churches in the United States took a stand against the Gulf War-I in 1991.

Pope Paul II and the Bishops of Southern Methodist Church (President Bush belongs to this church) opposed President George W. Bush's second war on Iraq in 2003.

In the long run, one has to sift through the debris of Haumain influences on religious organizations and revive the vision of spiritual practice. Once we understand the organizational dynamics, we can prevent the loss of vision. The time has come when the human consciousness has evolved to the point in which it can increasingly understand the Divine Order (Laws of Nature), make no punitive value judgments, and avoid the suffering created by the concept of sin. Instead of punishment, we can correct the situation with compassion and understanding.

hukme andar sabh ko, bahir hukam na koi
nanak hukme je bujhe tan haumain kahe na koi

Everything is in Divine Order nothing is outside of it.
Nanak, if one understands the Divine Order
Then one does not make haumain-based claims.
- Guru Nanak Dev ji, SSSG - P. 1

---

[3]My Sufi friend Sheik Mehmet Selim told me that the Muslims do no believe that Christ was crucified instead he ascended to heaven.

[4] Guru means a teacher. In Sikh scriptures Guru is also used for the Divine Enlightener. Bani is the Word Divine. Gurbani means Guru's word or verses.

[5]Gurdwara literally means Guru's Door. It is used for the Sikh place of worship where a Sikh passes through the threshhold to meet the Guru (the Divine Creator) by listening and understanding Gurbani. This understanding creates Naam consciousness (The Name or the Identity of the Creator) . The Sikh recites and sings Gurbani to meditate on Naam to merge with Naam.

I am attempting to take another look at the Sikh spiritual revolution that culminated in the manifestation of The Khalsa 300 years ago.

It was the culmination of more than 200 years of spiritual evolution in the northwest of India in Punjab state, a part of the Indus Valley civilization. It began with the birth of Sri Guru Nanak Dev ji in 1469. By the grace of Waheguru[6], he realized Waheguru within himself and in his presence everybody regardless of cast, creed or gender could experience the presence of Waheguru within. Bhai Gurdas ji described his birth on this planet:

satgur nanak pargatiya, miti dhundh jag chanan hoia

With the manifestation of the True Guru Nanak,
The mist vanished and the Light prevailed.
It was like the sun had risen.
The stars were hidden and the darkness vanished.
- Varan Bhai Gurdas, Var 1, P.27

Guru Nanak Dev ji examined every religious, social, economic and political institution through the spiritual eye and showed us the way to live in this world and be free of human suffering. He considered the greatest Yoga[7] and spiritual practice to be a householder with spiritual consciousness. It was the path of a karam[8] Yogi[9] who does not renounce the world but is not attached to his/her Haumain experiences. Nine Gurus succeeded him to provide a model of living through their thoughts, words and deeds. They created institutions to implement such a path.

The fifth Guru Sri Guru Arjan Dev ji, and the ninth Guru Sri Guru Tegh Bahadur ji gave their lives but would not budge an inch from their spiritual path.

On March 30 1699, it was the 10th Guru Sri Guru Gobind Singh ji who created Khalsa, the Sant Sipahi (Spiritual warrior). To fully appreciate this climactic creation, it is necessary to understand the evolution that resulted in the manifestation of the Khalsa. Sri Guru Gobind Singh ji, The Khalsa created Khalsa in his own image.

khalsa mero roop hai khas

Khalsa is my own true image.
- Sarab Loh Granth, Vol. 2, P. 531

This book is presented to readers who wish to find a living paradigm to alleviate personal suffering and contribute to peace on this planet. Some concepts and words may be quite difficult to comprehend because of the deafening noise of Haumain based religious, social, educational, business, economic and political institutions.

I have been teaching Gurbani to youth and children at the Sikh Center Gurdwara in El Sobrante, California since 1991. I asked the following

---

[6]Waheguru is Sikh name of the Divine. Wah is an exclamation in a state of awe and wonder of this beautiful and mysterious creation. Guru is the Divine Creator. Waheguru is an exclamation perceiving the Divine Naam in Its creation.
[7]Yoga: In the West it is commonly understood in terms of physical postures and meditation. The Sanskrit root is Yuj, meaning union, i.e., union with the Divine. It has the following components:
(i)Yama: Abstention from things like killing, untruths and thefts etc.
(ii)Niyama: Observance of purity, doing things in an orderly manner.
(iii)Tapas: Practice with concentration and practice of austerities.
(iv)Asnas: Yogic physical postures.
(v)Paranyama: Breathing exercises
(vi)Pratyahara: Shutting out all outward impressions and focusing the mind inward.
(vii)Dharana: Concentration on any one object.
(viii)Dhayana: Meditation
(ix)Samadhi: Final state of meditation when the subject of meditation and the object become one. - Courtesy of Kusum Bhat, Ph.D.
[8]Karama: Karama is usually translated as deeds. The worldly Karama are created by Haumain consciousness: Haumain Eha Jaat hai Haumain Karam Kamai (Haumain's nature is to create Karma). If one has no Haumain consciousness or attachment to it, one is liberated from Karma and is merged with the Divine while alive (Jeevan Mukt-achieves Moksha while alive).
[9]Karam Yogi is the one who lives as a householder and participates in all worldly affairs but is not attached to it and is free from it because one is steeped in the Divine.

23

question to the children at a junior high school age level at the end of the year: how do you recognize a Sikh? Their answers appeared in the following order:

1. One student said laughingly, you can recognize a Sikh by the long white kurta (robe), grey flowing beard and a staff in his hand.

2. You can recognize a Sikh by the five Ks: Kara(a steel bracelet), Kachh(shorts), Kes(unshorn hair), Kirpan(a sword bestowed upon the Sikhs to protect the unprotected), Kangha(a wooden comb for the hair).

3. A Sikh has a loving presence because he (she) has given up his (her) Haumain and lives in Naam[10] consciousness.

I would like to add a brief explanation to the third answer. Naam is the essence of all manifest reality in the Creation. The Creation runs according to the Laws of Nature (Divine Order-Hukam). Each of us is a part of this Cosmic Divine Order. The purpose of Sikh spiritual practice is to experience Haumain-based Karma, not get attached to the experience, and stay steeped in the Cosmic Divine Naam Reality.

The third answer made me feel that these little children at least intellectually understood what it means to be a Sikh. They could go beyond the appearances as Guru Nanak Dev ji taught us by criticizing the emphasis on appearance by the clergy of his time - the Brahmins and Mullahs. One of the Granthis[11] at the Gurdwara was initially quite skeptical about whether the children could grasp the meaning of Gurbani. I have been absolutely impressed by the sincere questioning of children and their understanding of Gurbani.

---

[10]Naam: The Divine identity that created everything. It manifests itself in it and is also transcendental.
[11]Granthi: The one who reads and interprets Sri Guru Granth Sahib, the holy book of the Sikhs.

Bana, the formal appearance of a Sikh or Khalsa is a gift to us from Sri Guru Gobind Singh ji. It was created so that the Sikhs could have the courage of their convictions and are willing to devote their life in loving devotion to Waheguru and Its creation - even if it means to sacrifice their life.

This book is written in appreciation of the children and youth at El Sobrante Gurdwara who have been a source of inspiration for me.

My translations of Gurbani are based on Punjabi translation by Dr. Bhai Sahib Singh (17), English translations by Dr. Gopal Singh (19) and UNESCO Collection (25). I have avoided using the words "God", "Lord", "Master", etc., and have kept the Gurbani names for the Divine. Poetic words evoke images and emotions historically associated with them. One can describe these words but cannot translate them without distorting the connotation of these words. I have also omitted the word Sikhism, because there is no such thing in Sikh spiritual practice. It limits and distorts what it means to be a Sikh.

I reorganized my presentation after receiving feedback from my friends. Initially, it began with the section on Evolutionary Process. It was suggested that I begin with the section on *A Sikh's Paradigm for Universal Peace*, because it introduces the basic concepts of Sikh Spiritual practice and the core theme of my intent. The reader may have an easier time following the rest of the text. It will still require your patience and help to accomplish this task. Even to the Sikh intelligentsia, people like me who are educated in the Western tradition, some interpretations may sound different and controversial. I would appreciate your feedback.

Some Sikhs may be struck by the encroachment of some superficial practices among the Sikhs, such as emphasizing form rather than substance, or making judgments about who is a better Sikh than someone else, setting oneself above the Sangat because of one's formal appearance. We may want to take another look and try to return to spiritual practice. I would appreciate your comments and feedback if you agree or disagree with my presentation or have additional comments.

If you fill out the feedback questionnaire and mail it to me or email at meji@pavior.com. I will be immensely grateful.

Thank you !

R.K. Janmeja Singh, Ph.D., Gyani

President

Ik Onkar Peace Foundation

IV

A Sikh's Paradigm For Universal Peace

Basic Concepts

IV.
A Sikh's Paradigm for Universal Peace

1. Sri Guru Granth Sahib, The Eternal Guru

The psycho-spiritual paradigm for peace and harmony is based on my understanding of Gurbani (Guru's word, the Sikh scriptures) and my experience as a psychologist. Therefore, I am going to summarize my findings in this section beginning with introducing Gurbani to you. The Divine verses (shabads) were collected by Guru Nanak Dev ji[1], Guru Angad Dev ji, and Guru Amar Das ji. The fifth Guru Sri Guru Arjan Dev ji preserved them in Sri Guru Granth Sahib ji. Gurbani consists of Divine hymns of 6 Sikh Gurus, 29 Bhagats (devotees) and Bards (Bhat) preserved in Sri Guru Granth Sahib ji. These exalted souls lived in spiritual consciousness, and Waheguru revealed Itself through them, and they wrote in that sublime consciousness. They were not only living models, but also described this consciousness and the experience of this world in their own words. This consciousness is embodied in Sri Guru Granth Sahib[2].

Imagine the difficult task I am given to describe Waheguru consciousness as revealed through beloved Gurbani. By necessity, I have to break down this introduction into different concepts, which destroys the beauty of the whole. It is like describing a person limb by limb, never capturing the beauty of the person's presence. I hope after understanding some of the basic concepts derived from Waheguru consciousness, the reader will enjoy the recitation of Gurbani and Kirtan in its original form, and experience the divine presence.

---

[1]Ji represents affectionate regard and respect for the person. It is usually used for elders or vernerale people like the Gurus.
[2]Sahib is an Arabic word also used as a mark of respect.

29

I attempted to describe the structure and content of Sri Guru Granth Sahib. An effort is made to explain some major concepts underlying the poetical expression in Gurbani. Near the end I share insights derived from my experience as a psychotherapist, mental health and organizational consultant. An effort is made to describe the similarities of the goal of my spiritual practice and the training to become an effective psychotherapist.. There is a discussion how these insights can lead to a paradigm that can bring peace and harmony in this world.

I hope to present a very brief outline of Gurbani consciousness using Gurbani's words and concepts, translating them freely. It is impossible to translate poetry from one language to another, and it is even more difficult when poetry emanates from a spiritual fountain head. Most of the translations at their best do not represent the beauty and subtleties of expression and the spirit embodied in it. At their worst they are inaccurate. To enjoy Gurbani fully, it has to be read in its original form and language.

Kapur Singh, M.A. (Cantab) M.P. describes the difficulties of translating Gurbani into English in his comments on Dr. Gopal Singh's translation (19) of Guru Granth Sahib as follows:

> "...The language and vocabulary of the Guru Granth is, therefore, connotative, associative and subjective, and the Guru-Granth deliberately, and by design, uses language not "purely" but ambiguously and thus, mostly, it is not the words and their conventional meanings that are of basic significance in the Guru Granth, unless the text is intended to be theoretical and prepositional, but the moss of meanings and associations and evocative power which the words employed have gathered around them throughout centuries of evolution and usage, by men who have experienced the non-verbal layers of reality. The poetic patina of the verbal vocabulary of the Guru-Granth does not necessarily have equivalences or correspondence in the cross vocabulary of the English

language. This renders the translation of the Guru-Granth more difficult than that encountered by Kumarjiva (4th C. Circa) while translating Mahayana texts into Chinese."

Those who are familiar with the Indian languages and cultural context may have direct access to this consciousness. **It will require as much effort on your part to learn a different experiential and conceptual framework, as it would be for me to use American conceptual and cultural context to bring these to fit into western context.** Since I spent the first quarter century of my life in India and more than four decades in the United States, I might serve as a liaison between the two worlds. However, there is no substitute for being in the actual presence of the Beloved.

oe bhi chandan hoe rahe base jo chandan paas

One who lives by the side of *Chandan* becomes *Chandan*
- Bhagat Kabir ji, SGGS - P. 1365

In a forest of a fragrant Sandlewood *(Chandan)* trees, every tree begins to have the fragrance of a *Chandan* tree. This metaphor is used to illustrate the effect of the presence of a person who is 'awake' and lives in spiritual consciousness. The Gurbani as written and compiled in Sri Guru Granth Sahib states that the presence of the Guru is in the Word, not in the physical form:

guru granth ji maneo pragat guran ki deh
jo prabh ko milbo chahe khoj shabad mein le

Consider Guru Granth ji as the body manifest of the Guru
Who so ever wants to meet the Guru can find It in the Word.
- Giani Gian Singh, Panth Prakash - P. 353

31

bani guru, guru aai bani vich bani amrit saare
gurbani kahe, sevak jan maane, partakh guru nistare.

The Word is the Guru and Guru is the Word
The Word has all the nectar of life

What the Guru says and the devotee incorporates it within oneself
The devotee experiences the manifest Guru within oneself.
- Guru Ramdas ji, SGGS - P. 982

The more frequently you meet a person and converse with them, the better you get to know them. To be lit up by Guru consciousness, one needs to meditate on the Word as much as possible. According to Sikh Rahit Marayada (14) the Sikhs are required to recite the following seven compositions every day.

Morning - Japji Sahib. Jaap Sahib. Anand Sahib. Sweyey - Pashahi ten and Benati Chowpaee
Evening - Rehras Sahib.
Night- Kirtan Sohila (before going to sleep)

The following practices contribute toward realizing the Sikh goal of perceiving Waheguru in everyone and merge with the Divine Cosmic Reality – Waheguru:

Meditation- Jap or Simran practice with a focus on and loving devotion to Waheguru Naam.
Sangat- Being in the company of saints or seekers.
Pangat: To partake and serve the blessed food in every Gurdwara to every one, regardless of caste or creed.
Dharamsaal: To provide free accommodation to pilgrims or travelers to a Gurdwara.

sat sangat kaisee janiye jithe iko naam vikhaniye

(The true Sangat is the one where only Naam is contemplated)

Kirtan- Singing of Shabads (Shabad literally means Word. These are verses from Gurbani)

Sewa: To be devoted to selfless and loving service of creation and fellow human beings.

Kirt: Earning with honest labor.

Vand Chhakna: Sharing your earnings with the needy.

sunia, mania, mann keeta bhao
antar gat tirath mal nahao

Listening to the Word, incorporating it within oneself,
Loving attachment to the Word
Through such internal pilgrimage, one cleanses oneself.
- Guru Nanak Dev ji, SGGS - P. 4

One does not have to judge oneself punitively because one has not attempted to realize Waheguru within oneself. It is also through Waheguru's grace that we are blessed to live in Waheguru consciousness. We cannot determine who is going to have a spiritual awakening, who is not, or when anyone's time comes to be merged with the One:

akhan jor chupe nah jor

It is not within human power to meditate
And develop Divine understanding.
It is not within one's power
To find the method of freedom from worldly bondage.
Waheguru, in whose hands the power is, exercises it,
Nanak, there is no one higher or lower then any one else.
- Guru Nanak Dev ji, SGGS - P. 7

The gifts are all divine,
The human is all too helpless.
Some do not receive them while awake,
Others are blessed by awakening them.
                    -Guru Nanak Dev ji, SGGS - P.83

All the above quotes indicate that Waheguru's *Hukam* (Divine Order) is the cause of everything. The question arises: if everyone does whatever Waheguru wills, then where is the freedom of will, personal responsibility, reward, punishment, sin, heaven and hell? These are very legitimate questions and pervade our consciousness today. To answer these and many more questions, I am called upon to write this book. After you study and not just read this book, please feel free to communicate with me. I am sure that the study of this book will answer some questions and raise many more. It may just be the beginning of a nice friendship and fellowship during our journey through this planet as Seekers (Sikhs). The Punjabi mystic poet Puran Singh wrote:

"People who reach a destination have a destination to reach."

2. Waheguru

Since I will introduce my beloved Gurbani as the living Guru of the Sikhs, it is essential to introduce to you its form, sources and some key concepts which are going to be used throughout this description (and are hard to translate).

Wah! is an exclamation in Punjabi. Whenever one sees something extraordinary, or listens to great music or poetry, one says Wah Wah! Guru literally means an enlightener. Gu means darkness, Ru means light. Guru is the one who removes the darkness and ushers in the Light. **"To teach any subject one has to know that subject. Since only the Creator knows about the Creation, only the creator can be the True Teacher. Sat Guru, Waheguru and Guru, are the words used for the Creator."** In general Guru has different meanings according to the context. Popularly it is used for a teacher or enlightener or the one who leads to Dharma.

Sat (Sanskrit Satya) means truth in Sanskrit, that which exists, which is Real. Therefore, "Satguru" is the one that is Real and exists forever, i.e. the Creator Itself. "Waheguru" expresses a state of mind created by the experience of wonders of creation, a loving appreciation of the creation, and a salutation to the Creator who manifests Itself in Its creation. Perceiving the Divine in everything, one exclaims Waheguru in loving salutation to this mysterious and beautiful creation. By meditating on Waheguru, one realizes oneself as a part of this cosmic play, and the sense of duality disappears.

balhari kudrat vasiya

I am a sacrifice unto You who resides in Nature (Creation)
It is impossible to describe your limits
Your Light pervades the Creation and
The Creation is contained in your Light
In mysterious ways You are perfection.
                              - Guru Nanak Dev ji, SGGS - P. 469

waheguru gurmantar hai, jap haumai khoi

Waheguru is Gurmantar
Meditating on it removes Haumain
                              - Bhai Gurdas ji, Var 13, 2

In Gurbani, Waheguru is the Gurmantar. In the ancient Indian spiritual literature, "Mantar" referes to a word or a phrase used to train one's mind

35

toward spiritual consciousness. Today, we have tools to make and fix things. It is quite extraordinary that thousands of years ago, Indian sages developed instruments and methodology to train one's mind and stay in a spiritually awakened state, remember the Source where we came from, and complete our journey in this body with a spiritual consciousness.

3. Gurbani

Gurbani refers to the poetical verses that come from the Source Waheguru. These are contained in Adi Granth, which the Sikhs call Sri Guru Granth Sahib, in reverence and respect for the scriptures. Guru Nanak called himself the Sikh of Satguru, the Creator.

> "Guru, the First Principle,
> The Pure one is in all things;
> Of this there is no doubt;
> Nanak has obtained the Creator;
> The Infinite Supreme Being as his Guru."

A Sikh is a seeker, a learner or a pupil. A human being that realizes Waheguru within himself/herself is recognized by the people who experience this presence.

> *braham gyani aap parmeshar*

> Says Nanak, a person who is enlightened
> by the Knowledge of Brahman
> (the Creator) is himself/herself Parmesher (Supreme Being).
> -Guru Arjan Dev ji, SGGS - P. 273

Traditionally, in Indian poetry the poet uses his/her name at the end of the poem. Since all the Gurus embodied Guru Nanak's spirit they used Nanak at the end of each verse. Outside of the Sikh gurus, only Mardana used

Nanak at the end of his verses. Guru Arjun Dev ji, while compiling Guru Granth Sahib used extra ordinary notations with each Bani to identify the *Raag* (musical form), the poetical form, the author and the number of the verse written in a long composition. For Example, *Gauri Deepki Mahla*-1. This title means that the verse was written by the first Guru Nanak (*Mahla*-1), and should be sung in *Raag Gauri Deepki*.

4. Compilation of Sri Guru Granth Sahib

Adi Granth was first compiled and edited by the fifth Guru, Sri Guru Arjan Dev ji and transcribed by Bhai Gurdas. Traditionally Sikhs believed that the first copy of the Adi Granth available at Kartarpur is written in his hand. The Dhir Mal family had the possession of the Adi Granth at the time of Sri Guru Gobind Singh ji. The Dhirmal family refused to hand over the Adi Granth to Sri Guru Gobind Singh ji. He dictated the whole Guru Granth Sahib to Bhai Mani Singh ji, assisted by Baba Dip Singh ji at Dam Dama Sahib, and added the Gurbani of the ninth Guru, Siri Guru Tegh Bahadur ji. Sri Guru Granth Sahib includes 1430 pages of poetry, mainly set to the Indian musical form of Raags. Innumerable poetical forms are used with metaphors of Punjabi farmers, Muslim, Hindu writings and love ballads of Punjabi literature. The Gurbani is written in Punjabi, Sanskrit, Farsi, Braj Bhasha, Marathi, and other Indian languages.

Gurinder Singh Mann in his book *The Making of Sikh Scriptures* states, "We have firm evidence that the hymns of Guru Tegh Bahadur were introduced into the Sikh text during his life time, that is, before 1675. G.B. Singh located a manuscript extant at Dhaka prepared in 1675, which contained all of Guru Tegh Bahadur's hymns recorded in their appropriate Raag and section." It is possible that Guru Gobind Singh ji had access to one of those copies when he prepared the final text of Sri Guru Granth Sahib and passed on the Guruship to Sri Guru Granth Sahib.

Sri Guru Granth Sahib contains the Bani of the first five Gurus, ninth Guru and the following 29 saints who were spiritually enlightened beings. They belonged to different religions and castes, were born in different parts of India, and wrote in their native languages. They ranged in life status from the cobbler Bhagat Ravidas ji to farmer Dhanna Bhagat to Raja Pipa Bhagat.

Sri Guru Granth Sahib ji is the embodiment of a spiritual consciousness that has no limits or boundaries created by regions, languages, religions or one's status in life. It is the manifestation of Waheguru who is infinite and has no limits or boundaries.

Following is the list of Bhagats (saints) whose Bani (verses) is included in Sri Guru Granth Sahib:

Bhagats
1. Kabir (1398-1448). He belonged to a recently converted Muslim weaver family. He is believed to be the disciple of Ramanand.
2. Sheikh Baba Farid (1170-1245), nephew of King of Ghazni, born in Khotwal near Multan in Punjab. His mother provided the chief religious influence on him. At age sixteen he went to Mecca. A few years later he adopted Qutab Din of Delhi as his Master (Pir). He was one of the first Punjabi Sufi poets.
3. Namdev (1220-1350), a tailor born at Narsi Bamni in Maharashtra. He spent about ten years in Punjab. He was a close associate of ascetic scholar Gyan Dev and the poetess Janabai. Sultan Mohammed Bin Tughlak imprisoned him, but he refused to give up his faith. He was set free when the Sultan became convinced of his spiritual greatness.
4. Ravidas (1450-1520) was a cobbler born in Uttar Pradesh. Members of highest caste became his disciples; prominent among them was princess Jhali of Chitore.

5. Ramanand (1366-1467), was born at Paryag near Madras, was the disciple of Raghvananda, the third in the spiritual descent from Ramanuja, quite early in his life settled in Benaras.

6. Parmanand (Fifteenth century) was a Brahmin Vaishnavite disciple of Ramanand who lived at Barei near Sholepur.

7. Sadhana (Fifteenth century) was a butcher of Sehwan in Sindh who made it a point to weigh meat he sold using an idol as a weight, thereby belittling idol worshop. Hated and condemned by Brahmins, he came to the Punjab where he probably met Namdev. He was bricked alive during the rule of the Sultans. His tomb is in Sirhind.

8. Pipa (1408-1468) was the ruler of Gagaraungarh State. He became a devoted disciple and friend of Kabir and Ravidas.

9. Sain (1390-1440), a court barber to the Prince of Rewa. He was touched by Ramanand and turned to Bhakti (spiritual devotion) and writing poetry. The prince was so impressed by his spirituality and wisdom, that he accepted Sain, the barber, as his Guru.

10. Sheikh Bhikhan (1480-1573), was a muslim Sufi saint, born in Luchnow who memorized Koran Sharif. He was strongly influenced by Kabir and Sufi disciples of Sheikh Farid.

11. Jaidev (1170-1245), the well known author of Gita-Govinda, a native of Kinduviloa in Birbhum district of Bengal, was the most distinguished poet in the court of Lakshman Sen, the last Hindu king of Bengal. The language of his hymns is a mixture of Prakrit and Apbhransh.

12. Beni (Ffteenth century), a contemporary of Namdev, a scholar and a poet with no livelihood. By strange circumstances, he was given an honorable post. He led a happy, saintly life.

13. Dhanna (Fifteenth century) was a farmer born at Dhuan in the State of Tonk near Deoli. The innocent peasant boy, seeing a Brahmin making a very comfortable living by merely worshipping an idol, also

sought the grace of the Creator by worshipping a stone. Krishna revealed Himself within him. He became the disciple of Ramanand.

14. Trilochan (1267-1335), a contemporary of Namdev, was initiated into mystic life by Gyan Dev.

15. Surdas (Sixteenth century), was a Brahmin saint whose scholarship and poetic talent won him the revenue officer position of Sandila, Oudh during the reign of Akbar the Great.

The Sikh Devotees

16. Mardana (1460-1530), a Muslim musician who played Rabab to the divine hymns of Guru Nanak. He accompanied Guru Nanak Dev ji on all his journeys, including to Mecca, Baghdad and other Middle Eastern places of pilgrimage. Other than the Sikh Gurus, Mardana was the only other person permitted to use Guru Nanak Dev ji's name to identify his verses.

17. Satta and Balwand were Muslim bards. Contemporaries of the second Guru Angad Dev ji, they were probably father and son. Very well versed in classical Indian music, they were employed by Guru Angad Dev ji thru Guru Arjan Dev ji to do Kirtan (Sing Gurbani)

18. Sunder (1560-1610), the great-grandson of Guru Amar Das ji.

Bhatts (The bard poets): All of the following are from the sixteenth century

19. Kalshar was the leader of ten other Bhats of Uttar Pradesh, who wrote about Guru Nanak Dev ji and successive Gurus from personal knowledge.

20. Jalap

21. Bhikhan

22. Salh

23. Bhal

24. Nalh
25. Gyan
26. Bal
27. Mathura
28. Kirat
29. Harbans

5. Ik Onkar

Sri Guru Granth Sahib begins with Ik Onkar. "Ik" means one. "Om" is the Creative force or the Creator. "Kar" means the physical form; Onkar, the one who is all pervasive.. Freely translated, it means that there is one Creator who is manifested everywhere and in everything.

Aapine aap sajio

It created Itself And Created Naam
Second created wonderful creation
Being in it enjoys Itself.
                              -Guru Nanak Dev ji , SGGS - P.463

The Mool Mantar; the Root Mantra describes some of the attributes of *Naam*, the Creator who is both immanent and transcendental.

Ik OnKar: Creator is One and all Pervasive
Sat Naam: Naam means name, the identity of the Creator. It is the consciousness of the Creator in its creation including human beings. Naam is the only Reality that exits. (The word Waheguru describes that consciousness).
Karta: Creator
Purkh: The Creative force
Nirbhao: Has no fear
Nirver: Has no enmity

Akal:	Beyond time, i.e., eternal
Moorat:	Form
Ajooni:	Does not go through the cycle of births and rebirths
Sehbhang:	Self-created
Gur Prasad:	You realize It through Waheguru's own grace.

-Sri Guru Nanak Dev ji, SGGS - P.1

The Sikhs strive toward realizing the eternal reality through meditation

Jap: Meditate

Aad Sach:	That existed before time
Jugaad Sach:	That has existed through all times (Yugas)
Hai Bhi Sach:	Exists now
Nanak Hosi Bhi Sach:	Nanak says, shall exist for all times to come.

Waheguru is one and is in everything. Its Name is the only realty that exists (all else is transitory). The Creator, who is fearless, has no enmity with anyone, is eternal and is Self created. One can realize Waheguru within oneself through Waheguru's own grace.

Meditate on the One who was there before the beginning, has existed through the ages, and is there now and will always be.

6. Creation

Let me begin with the beginning. The following is a description of what it was like before creation:

Arbad narbd dhandhukara

For aeons, there was nothing and there was neither earth
Nor the sky: only the Creator's Infinite Will was.
And there was neither night nor day, neither the sun nor the moon,
And the Creator was seated in Its Absolute Trance.

Neither there were the (four) sources of creation, nor of speech;
Neither air there was, nor water.
Neither birth nor death; nor coming nor going.
Neither division of the world there was, nor of the underworld,
Nor the seven seas, nor rivulets.
Neither was then the sky, nor the earth
Neither the world, nor the underworld;
Neither the celestial regions, nor the nether regions;
Neither death, nor time;

Neither being nor becoming, neither heaven nor hell,
Neither coming nor going.
Neither were there the Trinity of Brahma, Vishnu and Shiva;
No, there was none other but the One Absolute.
Neither woman then was, nor man:
Neither caste, nor station, neither pleasure, nor pain.
Neither there were the celibates, men of charity,
or the forest-dwellers;
Nor the adepts, nor seekers, nor indulgers in joys of the flesh;
Neither the Yogis, nor Jangams[1], nor Nathas[2], (any sect or creed).
Neither were practitioners of Austerities or Contemplation,
Nor of self-control, or worshippers, fasting men:

And, there was no one to utter, "Lo, there is also another."
The Creator only Itself was in Absolute Bliss and Prized only
It's Own Glory.

Neither Krishna, nor his consorts,
Neither the cows nor their herdsman;
Neither Tantra[3] nor Mantra[4] nor any deceptions,
nor any one played on the flute.
No one knew then the Way of works,
or the ever-buzzing fly of Maya[5]

---

[1]Jangam: Shivites, Shiva's devotees
[2]Nathas: Husbands or heroes
[3]Tantra: Rituals for protection or magical incantations
[4]Mantras: Words or sounds to train mind to be attuned to the Divine
[5]Maya: Transitory illusionary world created by Haumain consciousness.

Nor was attachment, involvement and death writ in any one's lot,
Nor any one neither contemplated nor knew whom to contemplate.
Neither there was slander nor rejection, neither life, nor body,
Nor Gorakha, the Guru of Yogis, nor Machhindra, his disciple,
Nor any thought or wisdom, nor the beginning of clans,
Nor was there the reckoning of the Account.
There were no distinctions of color, or coat, or of the Brah-
mins and the Kshatriyas;
Neither there were gods, nor temples, nor (the sanctity of) the cow,
Nor the recitation of the Gayatri[6]
Nor the offering to the sacrificial fire, not Yajnas[7]
Nor pilgrimages, nor worship (of the gods).
There were neither the Mullahs, nor the Qazis,
Neither the Sheikhs, nor the Hajis.
Neither the Kings, nor the subjects, nor the world of Haumain,
And no one there was to pride on one self.
Neither was there loving adoration (of the Creator),
Nor consciousness, nor unconsciousness:
And It Self was the Merchant and Itself the Peddler:
For, such was Its Will,
Neither there were the Vedas, nor the Semitic Texts,
Simritis nor the Shastras,
Nor the reading of the Puranas: neither the sunrise nor the sun-down,
The Creator, alone existed Itself remaining Unperceived,
Knowing only ItSelf unknowable Self.

When such was Its Will, It brought the Universe into being,
And without a seeming contraption, upheld Its Vast Expanse.
And Created Brahma, Vishnu and Shiva and
Instilled in humans the ever mounting desire for being attached.
But rare is the one whom the Guru (Creator) caused to hear Its
Word. For, the Creator Gave the Command and
Saw it happen and be all around
And (thus) It Created the entire universe
and its parts and the underworlds.

---

[6]Gaytry: It is the most sacred mantra of the Hindus
[7]Yajnas: Sacred fire rituals

44

And from the Absolute Self It Became Manifest.
No one knows the Extent of my Creator:
And, it is only through the Perfect Guru (the Creator)
That It is Revealed unto us.
Says Nanak: "They who are imbued with Its Truth are intoxi-
cated With Its Wonder: and thus wonderstruck, they sing ever
Its Praise.

-Guru Nanak Dev ji, SGGS - P. 1036-37

Guru Nanak Dev ji describes beautifully that before creation the Creator alone existed ItSelf remaining unperceived. It created everything
and became manifest in Its Creation and gave us Haumain to experience ourselves as a part of this creation and Naam to remember the
Source, the Creator, so that we do not get lost in this transitory existence of Haumain. He stated, "They who are imbued with Its Truth are
intoxicated with Its wonder: And thus wonderstruck, sing ever Its
praise." There are others who are caught in the Haumain based transitory reality and suffer by being preoccupied with duality, judgments,
rewards and punishment.

7.Naam

Naam literally means name. It is the identity of the Creator who is the
object of Sikh Meditation.

Aapine aap saajke

> The Creator created Itself
> And Created Naam (Name)
> Then created Nature,
> And abiding within it.
> Revelled in Its Wonder.

-Sri Guru Nanak Dev ji, SGGS - P.463

Its characteristics are described in **section 5. Ik Onkar,** and are repeated below:

The Creator is One and All Pervasive
Naam (Name) is the only Reality
The Creator,
Without fear,
Without enmity,
Beyond time.
Outside the cycle of birth and death,
Self-created.
One realizes It by the grace of Guru (the Creator) Itself.

Meditate
The Real Being existed before time
It existed through the ages
Nanak says, It will always be there.

-Sri Guru Nanak Dev ji, SGGS - P. 1

Furthermore:

Sargun Nirgun Nirankar

It has all the attributes.
It has no attributes.
It is formless.
It alone knows Itself.

-Sri Guru Arjan Dev ji, SGGS - P.290

Naam is the Name of the Creator. Everything we see around us is a manifestation of Naam. Naam is also the Divine Order. The creation functions according to the laws of Nature:

Naam ke dhaare sagle jant

Naam created all creatures.
Naam created all the worlds and universes.

46

Because of Naam are Smritis, Veds and Purans.
Because of Naam one meditates and has wisdom.
Naam created skies and underworlds.
Because of Naam there are all forms of life.
Because of Naam are continents and spheres.
Hearing Naam one is emancipated.
By Your grace the person who is blessed with Naam.
Nanak, that person reaches the highest stage of spiritual equa-
nimity and Bliss.

-Sri Guru Arjan Dev ji, SGGS - P. 284

Where does Naam reside? The Creator resides in all of us and the place
of Its abode is:

dinis na rein baid nahi shastar

Neither day nor night. Neither Vedas nor Shastras
That is where the Formless resides.

-Bhagat Kabir ji, SGGS - P. 484

Naam is transcendental as well as manifests It Self in Its Creation:

too parbraham parmesar

You are transcendental
You are outside of the cycle of birth and death
Your beauty is beyond description, how can we meditate on You!
You Your Self are in every one and manifest yourself in Nature.

-Sri Guru Arjan Dev ji, SGGS - P.1095

Naam is a part of the Divine Order:

sat sangat kaisi janiai

How do we know a Sat Sangat?
Where only Naam is recognized.

One Naam is Divine Order
Nanak, the True Guru has made me understand It.
-Sri Guru Nanak Dev ji , SGGS - P. 72

Satgur milia Jaaniai

When you meet a True Guru
You can discover Naam.
One recognizes a True Guru
Meeting whom you discover Naam.
-Sri Guru Nanak Dev ji, SGGS - P. 72

Naam is the Divine Order manifested in the Creation. One realizes it by understanding Gurbani, incorporating it, singing it and meditating on it. One's being begins to blossom with Cosmic Divine consciousness of Naam. Perceiving the mysterious beauty of creation, one exclaims Waheguru, Waheguru, Waheguru! The purpose of Sikh spiritual practice is to live in Naam consciousness. Each of us is a part of this Divine order. Therefore, making punitive value judgments is a reflection of "Ignorance." If one understands Divine Order, one is liberated from Haumain and the suffering caused by attachment to it. History is also an extension of Haumain and does not create a connection with the Cosmic Divine. To remove the veil of Ignorance (illusion of the transitory world), one needs to meditate on Naam.

The purpose of life is to experience life, not to make value judgments, but to remember our Source and become one with It while we are alive. This is achieved through loving devotion, selfless service of Waheguru and Its Creation. Realize that we are a part of this Cosmic Reality and are governed by the cosmic laws. Therefore, the sense of duality and making value judgments about oneself or someone else is a reflection of Haumain consciousness that creates duality. Re-

48

alizing the Divine within and Its Cosmic presence helps us attain the following state of Bliss:

na ko bairi na hi bigana

> The sense of enmity and estrangement is lost
> Since I have been in the company of saints. (Pause for reflection)
> Foe and stranger there is none.
> I am at peace with every one.
> Whatever the Beloved commands I accept with pleasure
> This is the wisdom I received from the saints.
> Waheguru resides in every one beholding It (in every one)
> Nanak is in a state of bliss.
>   -Sri Guru Arjan Dev ji, SGGS - P. 1299

Whenever we think of someone's name, it evokes certain thoughts and feelings, and conjures up images or attributes of the person associated with that name. The more deeply we meditate on Naam, the more Infinite images become a part of our consciousness and nothing looks different or strange. Naam is Nirankar (Formless), yet it is Sarabkar (has all the forms). The Creator is one and all pervasive; since the essence of everything is the Creator's spirit, everything in this universe is spiritual and sacred. All ancient people had this awareness, whether they were Native Americans experiencing the Great Spirit or people on other continents who attributed god names to its various manifestations in nature.

8. Process of Forgetfulness

The question arises: If the essence of all beings is the Creator Itself, then why is there so much "evil," destruction and suffering? To answer that question, one has to understand the "consciousness" process. There are two main kinds of consciousness in which humans live: Haumain (I am)

49

and, Naam (Creator) consciousness. Atman (the individual soul) is a fragment of Paramatma (the Supreme Soul) embodied in everyone. As soon as a person is born, a process of "forgetfulness" begins, described in the following verses:

Sri Raag Pahre.M.1

Pahle Pahre rein ke Vanjaaria Mitra

1. In the First Watch of the Night, you are cast into the womb,
O my Merchant-friend,
On your head (you stand) and do penance and
meditate on the Creator.
Yes, meditate you on your Creator, your mind fixed on It,
And then, naked are you delivered (into the world)
and naked again you leave it,
As is Writ on the Forehead, so is the working of one's soul.
Says Nanak: life in the First Watch,
is cast into the womb by the Creator's Will.
                    -Sri Guru Nanak Dev ji- SGGS - P. 75

In the First Watch of Night, your child-mind is unconscious,
Oh my Merchant-friend, You suck milk and are fondled,
And your mother and father love you for you are their son,
Your father and mother love you, their son, immensely,
but all attachment is Maya.
(But) without the Creator's name, you are saved not
And are drowned for your **Love of Duality.**
Says Nanak, " Man gets Deliverance in the First Watch
(only) by Dwelling on the Creator.
                    -Sri Guru Nanak Dev ji- SGGS - P. 76

dooje pahre rein ke vanjaaria mitra

2. In the Second Watch of the Night,
O my Merchant-friend, you forget your Creator.
From hand to hand you are danced about,

as Yashodha did with Krishna.
Yes, one is fondled and danced about,
and the fond mother says, "This is my son"
But, O my ignorant, unconscious mind,
in the end no one is yours.
You know not who willed the Creation,
nor gather Wisdom in yourself.
Says Nanak, "In the Second Watch of the Night,
one forgets (one's Creator)."

-Sri Guru Nanak Dev ji- SGGS - P. 76

In the Second Watch of the Night, the Wine of ripe beauty,
O my friend, intoxicates you!
Night and day, you indulge, and are blind to the Naam of the Creator.
All other tastes taste sweet to you
But the Creator's Naam is not in your heart.
You gather not Wisdom, nor the art of concentration, nor continence,
And so is your life wasted away.
By visiting the holy places, by fasting and cleansing the body
And performing the acts of piety
or the way of Karma one is emancipated not.
The deliverance, Nanak, is in the Loving Adoration of the Creator,
And all else leads to Duality.

-Sri Guru Nanak Dev ji- SGGS - P. 76

teeje pahre rein ke vanjaaria mitra

3. In the Third Watch of the Night,
your mind is fixed on beauty and riches,
O my Merchand -friend, you remember not the Creator's Name,
Through which one is delivered of one's bondage
In the Third Watch of the Night,
O my Merchant-friend,
the (white) Swans (of hair) descend on the pool (of your head).
Your youth wears out, and age is the winner
and your days grow less and less.
And then, at the end, you grieve,
When the Yama (the messenger of death) drives you blind-folded,

51

You kept all your goods to yourself as your own,
But in an instant they were all alien to you.
Your intellect left you, your wisdom departed,
And you repented for not remembering the Creator.
Says Nanak, "Fix your mind on the Creator,
in the Third Watch of the Night."

-Sri Guru Nanak Dev ji- SGGS - P. 76

Chauthe pahre rein ke vanjaaria mitra

4. In the Fourth Watch of the Night,
you get old and your body is shattered.
Blind-fold, you see nothing, nor your ears hear;
Your tongue loses its taste; lost are your activity and power.
How can he, who has no Virtue, get Peace;
the self-willed is born only to die.
When the life is ripe, it breaks with a click, and is destroyed,
How can then one be proud of mere coming-and-going?
Says Nanak, " In the Fourth Watch of the Night,
Know you the Word through the Guru.

And last comes the end of the breath, O my Merchant-friend,
For your shoulders are weighted down by cruel old age.
Not an iota of Good came into you, O my Merchant-friend,
And bound down by Ignorance,
You are driven along.
He who goes the Way of Remembering Divine
And Continence is hurt not and ceases his comings-and-goings.
Neither Death, nor Maya's snare is for him,
For he swims across (the Sea of
Fear and Suffering) with Love and Devotion.
He goes with Honor, is Merged in the Great Peace,
And all his Woes depart.
Says Nanak, "Man is saved by Truth and
Through Truth does he receive Honor."

-Sri Guru Nanak Dev ji- SGGS - P. 77

We are totally lost in the Haumain consciousness. We get attached to the transitory objects (object relations theory talks about the transitory object, like a teddy bear, that serves as a substitute for the real love object which are the parents of the infant). What we do not realize is that all our relationships in the manifest world are also transitory objects. The Ultimate Love object is the Source from which we came. But we forget it and get attached to our individual identity (Haumain) and all its extensions.

We feel the losses of these Haumain-based attachments because we lost touch with the Source, the True Love Object. The first step to spiritual awakening is Vairag (longing for the Beloved).

9. Vairag

The longing for the Beloved Waheguu is a state of Vairag. Haumain pursuits put us to sleep and we forget our True Identity and Waheguru. Love is the way to realize the beloved within oneself. The separation from the Beloved creates Vairag state.

Ik ghari na milte

> If I am not with you for a moment
> It is like being in dark ages (Kal Yug)
> When will I meet you my venerable Beloved?
>   Sri Guru Arjan Dev ji, SGGS - P.96

Vairag is the sign of spiritual awakening. One can also measure one's own spiritual awakening by the intensity of Vairag, longing for the beloved. Intellectual understanding and discourse is not the way one merges with the Beloved. If anything, it can keep us away. Spirituality is a matter of heart and soul, not of head and intellect.

Spiritual beings such as Guru Arjan Dev ji, Guru Tegh Bahadur ji, Jesus Christ and many other Bhagats and saints who sacrificed their lives were not guided by their intellect, but by their love of Waheguru. Our intellect always misguides us by weighing what is in our personal, community and national interest. Only the love in our heart like the *Panj Payare* (The Five Beloved Ones) enables us to sacrifice our life to protect others.

Jaa bhao paa-e apna bairag upjai man aa-e

When there is love within,
Vairag captures one's mind
Through Vairag one realizes
Waheguru and one merges with It.
Sri Guru Amar Das ji, SGGS - P. 490

Satgur Saven so vadhbhagi

Those who serve Satguru are fortunate
Those who love True Shabad (Gurbani)
Those who are householders with family,
Yet are in a Sehaj (state of spiritual equanimity) meditation.
Nanak, who are drenched in Naam are true Vairagi (Bairagi).
Sri Guru Ramdas ji, SGGS - P. 1246

10. Jeevan Mukt (Achieving Moksha While Alive)

Indian religious traditions stem from concerns about the suffering in this world. They emphasize understanding the causes of this suffering and how to be emancipated from this suffering to achieve a state of Jeevan Mukt-Salvation, Moksha or emancipation while one is still alive.

The death of Haumain attachment liberates us from suffering. The Waheguru or Naam consciousness of a Gurmukh and attachment to Haumain consciousness of a Manmukh is described in the following pages.

11. Manmukh And Gurmukh

Manmukh: Attachment To Haumain
Gurmukh: Loving Devotion to Divine

People who are "awake" and have not forgotten the source (Supreme Soul -Param Atma) are not attached to this transitory world that is constantly changing. Manmukh lives in an illusion regarding this material world (Maya) as Real; that our body, mind, things and people are Real and will be there forever. The only Reality that exists forever is the Divine and Its Creation. A **Gurmukh** is the one who is blessed to remember the Creator and the Source one came from. **He/she sees the Creator in its Creation and experiences him/herself as a part of it, and is in an eternal state of bliss.**

MANMUKH: HAUMAIN ("I am" consciousness)
Guru Nanak Dev ji describes the characteristics of Haumain as follows:

Saloak M. 1:

>*Haun vich aya haun vich gaya*

    In Haumain one comes: in Haumain one goes.
    In Haumain is one born: in Haumain one dies.
    In Haumain one gives, in Haumain one takes.
    In Haumain one earns, in Haumain one wastes.
    In Haumein is one truthful or lies like a liar.
    In Haumain one reflects on Virtue and Sin.
    In Haumain do we land in heaven and hell.
    In Haumain are we happy, in Haumain sorrow.
    In Haumain do we sin, in Haumain we wash it off.
    In Haumain do we lose the distinction of caste and creed.
    In Haumain are we wise; in Haumain are we unwise.
    Yes, in Haumain is our birth upon birth.

If one spots out the Haumain within,
one arrives at the Gate (of Deliverance).
**But without enlightenment, one argues
and fights worldly duels in vain.**
Nanak; Through the Creator's will is the making of our Destiny,
And as It sees us, so should we see ourselves.

-Sri Guru Nanak Dev ji, SGGS - P.466

M.2

Haumain eha jaat hai, haumain karam kamai

The nature of Haumain is to create Karma.
The bondage of Haumain is that
we are bound to the cycle (of birth and death)
How is Haumain born? In which way is the Release?
Yes, this is the Creator's Will that, in Haumain,
one follows the Writ of habit.
Haumain is a chronic malady but within it also is its remedy.
If the Creator be in Grace,
one practices the Word of the Guru (Creator).
Says Nanak: "Hear you humans, thus is this malady cured".

-Sri Guru Angad Dev ji, SGGS - P. 466

Sometimes Haumain is translated as ego. There are value judgments attached to ego, whereas Haumain has no value judgment. I have to have "I am" consciousness to experience the world. It only brings suffering when I get attached to the experience and forget the Divine within me.

Our Karmic life is based on Haumain consciousness: good-bad, evil-virtue, right-wrong are a reflection of Haumain reality. Sin, hell, and heaven are all manifestations of Haumain consciousness. Many of the value judgments are a part of this reality. Karma is usually translated as deeds. They can be good deeds or bad deeds. In the above context our **experience** of Karma is only possible as long as there is Haumain.

For example if you abuse me, I may feel hurt or anger. What is this **"I"** that feels hurt or rage? This is my Haumain consciousness that experiences it. My reaction will depend on the nature of my Haumain and the intensity of my attachment to it.

We become attached to our body, thoughts, feelings, possessions, and relations, and we begin to differentiate me and mine, from you and yours. Haumain creates a sense of duality and one makes value judgments.

Bura bhala tichar akhda

Bad and good one says as long as
there is a sense of duality (created by Haumain)
A Gurmukh realizes the Only One and merges into the One.
-Sri Guru Amar Das ji

Haumein gives us the pleasure of our possessions and achievements, including the achievement of a virtuous life. This can lead to pride:

tirath barat ar daan kar

"Holy pilgrimage, cleansing fasts, charity and virtuous deeds;
If these create pride in mind, Nanak, these are as useless, as
bathing an elephant."
-Guru Tegh Bahadur ji, SGGS - P.1428

We also suffer pain when we are rejected, fail, or lose our possessions or loved ones. A **Manmukh** (driven by his/her mind in Haumain consciousness) follows the dictates of his/her mind, becomes attached to Haumain, lives in this transitory reality (Illusion-Maya) and suffers. The more deeply we are attached to Haumain("I am"), the more the self-created shackles around us squeeze us tightly, and the more intense is our suffering. (Please see Illustration I & II).

Manmukh and Gurmukh are not mutually exclusive. Both Manmukh and Gurmukh live in the same Maya world. The difference is created by how much the person is attached to one's Haumain or how much one lives in loving Divine consciousness. All of us exist on this continuum. As an example, on one end of this continuum is Guru Nanak-Guru Gobind Singh and on the other end is Emperor Aurangzeb. A summary of the difference in their behavior reflecting different consciousness is give on pages 210-212. Other examples are Christ vs. the Romans; Muhammad vs. the Mecca power elite. Sri Guru Amar Das ji states that a person who stays steeped in the love of the Divine can realize It within oneself and merges with It while living in this Maya world.

Jesi agan udar mein tesi

As is the fire of the womb within,
So is the fire of Maya outside.
Both fires are alike.
Both are part of the Divine Creation.
According to Divine Will one is born
To the great joy of one's family and
Love for the Divine is lost.
Lustful pursuits of Maya take over,
This Maya makes one forget the Divine (also see pages 44-46),
Attachment is born and one is attached to other (then divine),
Nanak says, by the grace of Waheguru
One who stays steeped in the love of Divine,
Can find Divine within Maya.
                    -Sri Guru Amar Das ji, SGGS, P.921

In my observation of psychopathology, I find the intensity of Haumain attachment is directly proportionate to the intensity of one's suffering during infancy. One develops unique ways to cope with the pain, and continues to create an environment in which one suffers when one is an adult. Most people identified as suffering from borderline personality disorders have been sexually or physically abused, recreate abusive relationship in their adult life and suffer intensely through out their life. One should not make punitive value judgments on their apparent behavior but try to understand and heal the underlying pain that they suffered in their infancy or child-hood (also see pages 69-82).

Haumain based reality is not unreal or false. The Creator created it to experience It Self. It leads to suffering only when we live in Haumain consciousness and become attached to the reality created by it, forget the Source, become blind, and cannot see the same spirit manifested in this Karmic World. Manmukh (a person who follows the dictates of the mind) consciousness is influenced by the mind. This mind contains the following five impulses that distract him/her from Waheguru.

1. Moh: Attachment
2. Kaam: Lust
3. Krodh: Anger (Hatred).
4. Lobh: Greed
5. Hankar: Pride

Guru Nanak raises the question:

Kiv sacheara hovia

How can one realize Truth (what is Real and Exists for ever) and break down the wall of falsehood, the unreal?"

He answers:

Nanak says, if one accepts the Divine Order
and surrenders to the Will of the Creator,
It will accompany you
(to the door of deliverance from suffering)
                                    -Sri Guru Nanak Dev ji, SGGS - P.1

Through enlightenment one engages in **Meditation Karma.**
Once enlightened one is Liberated of Karma."
                                    -Bhagat Ravidas ji

Gurmukh: Naam or Divine Consciousness

The Enlightened person is liberated from this Karmic life while still alive because of detachment from Haumain. In most cultures, the lotus is a symbol of spirituality. The lotus has its roots in the mud and gets its energy from it, but rises above it and is not affected by it. Similarly, a spiritually enlightened being experiences Haumain based deeds and all the emotions aroused by such experiences, but is not attached to them. In the following verse, Guru Nanak Dev ji describes that everything is in a state of Divine Order and there is nothing outside of It.

Hukmi hovan akar

By Divine Order, all forms come into being
This Order cannot be described
(because it is so far above our understanding)
By Divine Order, the creatures came into being
By Divine Order, some are given high status
Because of the Divine Order, some have high or low status
Because of the Divine Order, some suffer, and some are happy
Because of the Divine Order, some are liberated and others are caught (in Maya)
Everyone is subject to Divine Order, no one is outside of It
Nanak, if one understands this,
Then one would not assert one's Haumain.
                              -Sri Guru Nanak Dev ji, SGGS - P.1

If all of us are a part of the Divine Order, then I am not the cause nor am I the creator of my own destiny. Therefore, one experiences the Karmic reality with detachment and one is not affected by one's Karmic life:

Je sukh deh ta tujhe aradhin

"If you give me comfort I recite your name
In suffering I still meditate on you!"
                              -Sri Guru Ramdas ji, SGGS - P.757

Since everything is in Divine Order, even the understanding of this Divine Order and becoming enlightened is not because of one's personal efforts, it is by the Grace of Waheguru. Therefore, one cannot even be proud of one's enlightenment if one is truly enlightened:

Aakhan jor chupeh na jor

(I have) no power to speak, or to do meditation.
Nor (do I have) power to collect wealth and rule,
Nor the power to control the disturbed mind.
(I have) no power to awaken the soul
To reflect on the Divine Knowledge;
Nor the power to find the way
To get release from the bondage.
The One, who has the power, exercises it,
Nanak: None is high or low."
-Sri Guru Nanak Dev ji, SGGS
- P.7

Karan kaaran samrath hai

Nanak has realized that the Divine
Has the power over deeds and causes
Cause is in the hands of the Creator
Who created it all.
-Sri Guru Nanak Dev ji, SGGS - P.149

The whole idea of surrender to God's will, Allah's Raza and Waheguru's Bhaana, is to understand the Divine Order and become non-attached to haumain and its illusionary creation Maya. I am not the doer and I am not the cause. I am a part of this Divine Order. There is a total surrender to the Will of the Divine. Therefore, one does not make punitive value judgments on oneself or others' behavior because we are all a part of the same Divine Order. A Gurmukh tries to **understand** the pain of other people and finds ways to heal it. When Christ

61

was crucified he said, "Father, forgive them **for they know not what they do.**" They were a part of the Divine Order. The way to liberate them of their Karma is through **understanding and not through punishment.**

By the grace of Waheguru, a person may pursue the path of a Gurmukh or a Gursikh. A GurSikh gets up early in the morning (Amrit Vela, three hours before dawn), takes a shower or bathes himself, and he/she meditates on Naam (Simran). Then he/she also does Nit Neim (daily practice) as described on page 32.

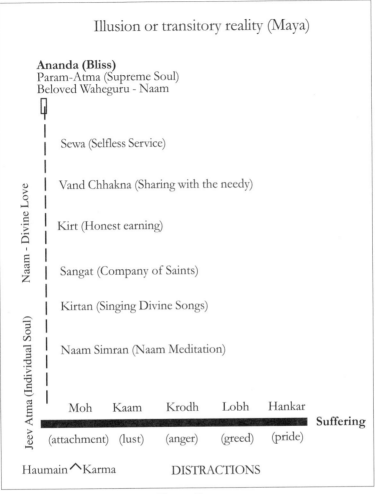

Figure - I

The dotted lines indicate a weak connection with Waheguru (Creator). A solid line indicates a strong attachment to transitory illusionary world (Maya), and its extensions Kaam, Krodh, Lobh, Moh and Hankar that leads to suffering. Haumain creates Karma. If there is no Haumain, then there is no Karma.

Gurmukh

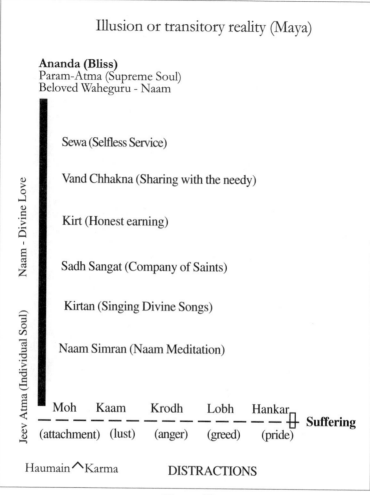

Figure - II

The dotted lines indicate a weak connection with attachment to transitory illusionary world (Maya) and its extensions Kaam, Krodh, Lobh, Moh and Hankar that lead to suffering. Again, Haumain creates Karma and if there is no Haumain then there is no Karma. There is an eternal state of bliss. The solid dark line indicates strong, devotional Love connnection with Naam (Beloved Waheguru) and the practice of Naam Simran, Kirtan, Sadh Sangat, Kirt, Vand Chhakna and Sewa leads to bliss (ananda).

12. Ardas (Prayer)

Most of the Sikh spiritual practice is a devotional meditation to realize the Cosmic Divine within, to merge with the Beloved and alleviate a sense of duality. It could be the recitation or singing of Gurbani, or meditation on Sat Naam or Waheguru. Ardas is a meditation and a prayer to the Divine for guidance and blessings. The first part is visualizing and meditating on the teachings and deeds of the ten Gurus who are a Sikh's spiritual support. The next part is to remember and meditate on those who lived in Naam consciousness and sacrificed themselves, but did not stray from love of the Divine and the righteous path. The last part is asking for blessings.

At the end of every Sikh religious ceremony, the Sadh Sangat (the companionship of the saints) stands with folded hands facing Sri Guru Granth Sahib. It is also recited by every Sikh after he/she completes the morning recitation, evening recitation and nightly recitation of Gurbani. There may or may not be the presence of Sri Guru Granth Sahib. When a Sikh is in doubt, or is starting a new venture and needs guidance and spiritual support, the Sikh does the Ardas before Sri Guru Granth Sahib and then opens Sri Guru Granth Sahib to receive Hukam Naama (the message) or Vaak (Guru's Word). In the morning after opening Sri Guru Granth Sahib at random, a Sikh reads the verse on top of the left page. If it begins on the previous page, it is read from that page and ends on the top of the left page. At the end of the day before Sri Guru Granth Sahib is closed and put to rest, the Sikh reads the Vaak from the top of the right page unless the verse starts on the left page; then it is read starting on the bottom of the left page and ending on the top of the right page.

Description of Ardas Ceremony: One Sikh leads the Sangat and everyone sings the following *Sloak*:

Too Thakar Tum Peh Ardas

You are my deity and I pray before you,
By your grace my body and mind are well
You are my mother and father, and we are your children
Because of your grace
I have boundless Peace and comforts
Nobody knows Your limits, You are higher then the highest
You alone know the mysteries of Creation,
Nanak is an eternal sacrifice unto You.

The Sikh, leading the Ardas, starts by reciting some sloaks while the rest of the Sangat is quietly attuned to him/her. The sloaks are not a part of the original Ardas. They are optional and are selected by the person who is leading the Ardas:

Tud Aage Ardas Hamari Jeeo Pind Sabh Tera

I am doing Ardas before you,
the body and soul are all Yours
Nanak says it is all Your greatness, nobody knows my name.

Vin Tud Hoar jo Mangna[1]

Asking for anything other than You
Is a suffering beyond any suffering
Gift of Your Naam has satiated me
And my mind's hunger is no more

Ardas

There is one Creator who is all pervasive
Victory to Waheguru ji.
May the Supreme Being be my support.

Ballad of the Supreme Being written by
the tenth Guru Sri Guru Gobind Singh ji.

Pauri[2]

Meditate on the Supreme, then meditate on Nanak
Then Guru Angad and Guru Amar Das, they are my support
Then meditate on Arjan , Har Gobind and Sri Har Rai
Meditate on Sri Harkrishan, seeing him all the suffering vanishes
Meditating on Guru Tegh Bahadur brings nine treasures home,
May they support us everywhere,
May the tenth Guru Gobind Singh Sahib ji be our support everywhere,
Visualizing the Light of the ten Gurus Sri Guru Granth Sahib,
Its presence and recitation of Gurbani say Waheguru, Waheguru, Waheguru!
(The Sangat says Waheguru along with the Sikh leading the Ardas)

Contemplating on the five Beloved[3] ones,
The four sons (of Guru Gobind Singh ji), forty Liberated[4] ones,
Those who were steadfast, meditators and self-disciplined,
Meditated on Naam, shared their earnings, started Langar
And wielded sword (to protect the unprotected),
Those who overlooked short comings,
Visualizing the deeds of those Beloved and True ones
Khalsa ji say Waheguru, Waheguru , Waheguru!

Those Singh men and women who sacrificed for righteousness
Were broken on the wheel, their bodies were sawed, were flayed alive.
Those who sacrificed in the service of Gurdwaras,
did not abandon the righteous path
Practiced Sikhi donning hair to the last breath.
Visualizing their deeds, Khalsa ji, say Waheguru, Waheguru, Waheguru!
Visualizing the five seats of Sikh religious authority

---

[1] Sri Guru Angad Dev ji, SGGS - P.959
[2] Pauri: a poetical form
[3] Beloved Ones: the five persons who offered to sacrifice their lives in order to receive
Amrit (nector of eternity)
[4] Forty Liberated Ones: Forty persons had given in writing that they were
no more Guru's Sikhs. Later on they sacrificed themselves in fighting against the
tyranny of Aurangzeb

And all Gurdwaras, please say Waheguru, Waheguru, Waheguru!
The Primal Supreme, this is the prayer of the entire Khalsa
May entire Khalsa remember Waheguru, Waheguru, Waheguru
Through this remembrance, may there be peace and joy.

Wherever there is Khalsa ji, there and everywhere
they receive Your protection.
May the Langar and sword prevail
Preserve the honor of your devotees
Bestow victory on the Panth[3].
May the Supreme Spiritual sword be an assistance,
May Khalsa always gain honor, say Waheguru, Waheguru, Waheguru!

Give Sikhs the boon of Sikhi, of preserving hair,
Observing the Sikh code of conduct and Divine wisdom
Boon of trust, of faith, the supreme boon of Naam
And bathing in the pool of eternity.
Kirtan, flags and shrines may last through the ages
May righteousness triumph, say Waheguru, Waheguru, Waheguru!

May the mind of the Sikhs be humble and their wisdom profound
Waheguru Itself is the protector of wisdom
O Eternal Giver always provide support to
Your organization of devotees
O, the Honor of the humble, Might of the powerless
Support of the supportless, the True Father Waheguru
In your presence we have prayed for (insert the occasion of Ardas)

O True Father forgive our mistakes in reading Gurbani or doing Kirtan
Fulfill every one's endeavors
Give us the company of those beloved ones
Meeting whom we remember Your Naam
Remembering Nanak and Naam, May everyone be in high spirits
By Your Will may every one be blessed.
>   *Waheguru Ji Ka Khalsa Waheguru Ji Ki Fateh!*

---

[5]Panth: Sikh community and khalsa organization.

(If there is a Sangat where Prasad and Langar has to be served. The following lines are added)

The True Father, Waheguru, in your presence is placed
The Karrah Prasad from the Sadh Sangat
And food from Sadh Sangat's Langar, May it be accepted by You
May the accepted Karrah Prasad and Langer be distributed in the Sadh
  Sangat
Whoever partakes, may he/she recite Your Naam with each breath
Those beloved devotees who have done
Sewa in preparing the Prasad and Langar
Bless them with happiness, peace and the gift of Your Naam!

At the end of Ardas there is a recitation of a few more Sloaks followed by a Jaikara (melodious beckoning of victory).

> Bhai ji says
>> *Jo Bole So Nihal*
>>> (Whoever says gets joy of fulfillment)
> The Sangat responds
>> *Sat Sri Akal!*
>>> (Truth, The Supreme and Eternal)

13. Hukam: The Divine Order

PERSONAL RESPONSIBILITY AND SIN

A Psychological Perspective

It is hard to believe in divine order when every day we make choices. We 'choose' our clothes, careers, partners, friends and schools. We experience making choices, but we do not actually determine our choices. Each choice is determined by very complex factors. I share with you my experience as a psychotherapist and a mental health consultant to elaborate on the complexity of factors that determine our choices. Hukam (Divine Order) is as applicable to human behavior as it is to physical sciences.

Instead of developing an elaborate discussion regarding 'choice,' I want to mention the Rorschach Inkblot test. A psychologist shows an inkblot to the person and asks, "What does it look like?" Each person chooses to respond any way they want, and everyone sees different things in different parts of the inkblot. On the basis of these responses, a psychologist develops a picture of the intra-psychic processes of the person, which determined their responses.

How free is the person if the unconscious intra-psychic processes determine their choices? Those processes are further determined by the influences the person experienced in his/her infancy and life-long developmental process. Moreover, those experiences are determined by genetics, socio-economic status, and the cultural and political context in which they grew up. **There is an "experience" of making a choice, I experience making that choice but it is not determined by me.** A highly complex process determines my choices, but I believe "I" chose to marry, "I" chose to suffer through divorce, "I" chose to murder, rape and cause suffering, "I" chose to do good deeds. Such a belief approaches close to a delusion because it is so far from reality.

To liberate ourselves from inflicting pain on others and ourselves, is to understand the Divine Order. All spiritual beings throughout history surrendered their attachment to Haumain and lived in Unconditional Love for Divine and Its creation.

To some extent, we experience this non-attachment in the psychotherapy relationship. The patient "transfers" his/her unconscious sense of being to the therapist. The therapist experiences thoughts, feelings, emotions and temptations (curiosity, sexual, sad or angry feelings, positive and negative impulses), but does not see them as "real." (They are aroused by the Haumain based karmic reality of the patient and the therapist. They are

Maya, an illusion). He/she does not react to the "reality" created by the patient in a therapeutic relationship. The therapist does not use the patient for personal gratification (renounces Haumain based satisfaction) even though she/he experiences sexual or angry emotions or the temptation to react to the patient. On the contrary, the therapist remains focused on the suffering of the individual as a result of his/her Karmic Haumain identity and karmic environment. (See pages 55-65 for more explanation of Haumain and Maya)

The therapist comes from a place of Love, unconditional acceptance, and regard for the individual's experience. The therapist does not make punitive value judgments and uses his/her knowledge of intra-psychic, interpersonal, family, socio-political dynamics and economic context to avoid getting trapped in the intra-psychic reality of the individual. **As a patient becomes more comfortable in the unshakable loving presence of the therapist, he/she begins to have the courage to re-experience in a detached way the pain and suffering caused by the Karmic environment. Through self-reflection and an inward journey, the individual becomes liberated from his/her infantile Karmic conditioning, and begins to develop a different sense of himself/herself and other people around him/her.**

This is accomplished through the total detachment of the therapist from Haumain (I am), and by not using the patient for impulse gratification of any kind. The therapist does not satiate his or her psychological needs and insecurities through the relationship with the patient. **To become a therapist, one has to constantly renew one's ability to "love" and practice Haumain detachment through constant self-reflection, meditation, peer support or supervisory support and understanding the complexities of human behavior and motivation. During such a process, the client also becomes more detached from the Haumain**

Karmic experience established during infancy, and its impact on the client's life. The client will progress toward realizing his/her True Identity, the Source, to the extent that the therapist has realized his/her True Identity. Such a state of being is consistent with the spiritual sense of being.

In 1963, I had the privilege of spending a year with Prof. Gerald Caplan, considered the father of Preventive Psychiatry, and a teacher of Community Mental Health Consultation at Harvard School of Public Health. He found that one could alleviate the unconscious interference in a problematic interaction in one or two sessions. During the last forty years of my practice, I have built on that notion, and developed technology that I use in couples and family therapy, supervision, administration and organizational consultation. The same loving and non-judgmental attitude is as helpful in the above situations as it is in individual psychotherapy. The emphasis is on understanding rather than indulging in finding fault. **The consultant uses one's knowledge of intra-psychic, interpersonal, group, organizational and community dynamic processes to identify the most important issues, and focuses the discussion where it will have the most impact. One uses such knowledge to ask questions that will elicit the most relevant information for developing an objective and comprehensive understanding in order to alleviate the distress.** Through my organizational consultation experience, it became quite obvious to me that the individuals within an organization are not the determining factors regarding what happens in that organization. To be useful as an organizational consultant, one has to look at the pressures impinging on the organization and its ability to resolve those pressures in terms of the structures and processes available to the organization (23). It is also true of inter-national conflicts.

I tried to use my psychological knowledge and skills, and elements of my spiritual practice in the administration of The Hume Center. In order to implement an empowerment paradigm instead of an evaluative punitive model of administration and to create a supportive environment, I summarized my expectations in the welcome letter as the Director of the Center in the following paragraph:

"We have evolved guidelines, based on our understanding of the therapeutic process, to help one another as we work toward realizing our highest potentials. In our relationships with each other we are courteous and friendly, avoid making derogatory comments, look for opportunities to be helpful, avoid getting hooked into the negative aspects of our colleagues, promote the positive, ask clarification questions rather than responding with quick reactions and value judgments, communicate directly with the person involved, and give unconditional love and service before self. In relation to our working together, we act according to our role and play according to the rules, meet work deadlines and stay task-focused, follow channels of communication in decision making, and use a problem-solving focus rather than fault finding."

The above letter created a common reference point. Fortunately, the staff, interns and post-doctoral fellows who come to the Hume Center are aware of the spiritual nature of the journey on this planet. By the Grace of the Divine we all work toward an atmosphere of peace and harmony within a supportive therapeutic environment in order to maximize the recovery of our patients from emotional suffering and mental disorders.

The process of forgetfulness of Waheguru begins to take place from birth. Our consciousness begins to be shaped by the experiences of embodied Jeev Atma (soul) in relationship to the environment. Psychologists have studied this process quite extensively. In our clinical experience, we observe that the individuals who have lived in an oppressive emotional environment, or have been emotionally, physically or sexually abused, lose their connection with Param Atma or Cosmic consciousness, and withdraw into themselves. They become very suspicious of the world around them. Children who are beaten and punished may become anti-social personalities, as well as rapists and murderers.

Parents who abuse their children were abused themselves as children. If we want our children to be loving individuals, then we have to cultivate this loving spirit within ourselves. Parents should not be blamed for abusing their children because our religious, academic, business, social and political institutions are based on Haumain consciousness and create an environment of desperation.

We glorify people who plunder and murder other people for their individual, community or national interest. We call them brave conquerors and heroes. We try to eternalize them by building statues of them and writing books about their exploits. History is a perspective and reflection of our consciousness. Recently, some people have begun to realize how inhuman we have been to each other in the name of religion or vested national interest. Our national leaders apologized for the atrocities committed against Japanese or Afro-American slaves. Professor Zin's *People's History of the United States* is another example of seeing history from the victim's perspective. **There is a danger that people who were victimized become perpetrators when they assume power.**

These things will continue to happen as long as we glorify Haumain based actions. We are "attached" to ourselves as individuals, to our communities, or our religious and national identities. These are all an extension of Haumain. A person who is connected with Waheguru perceives Waheguru in everyone and serve everyone instead of exploiting others for their own individual, community **or** national interest. Like Bhai Kanahiya (page, 193

A True Sikh), sees Waheguru in everyone. Then how can he/she exploit others and cause suffering? Our institutions perpetuate and glorify competition, individual achievement, greed and exploitation.

In Punjabi, "maya" has two meanings: Maya means wealth, it also means the Illusionary, unreal, transitory world. We are so caught in the Haumain based institutions that we cannot even consider another paradigm of co-operation, sharing, loving, caring and service.

Parents who are abusive toward their children are not only impelled by their infantile experiences, they also can be victims of the pressures created by the **Haumain based system around them. We may be too caught in our material pursuits** - either we are too poor or too greedy. We may be too attached to our expectations of our children. Any violation of our expectations can result into a **violent response towards our children. Sometimes, our violence toward our** children may be an expression of our helplessness to deal with the interaction, or, it may just be an expression of the unbearable pressures within ourselves.

Adults who have become dangerous to themselves or others need to be in a protective, but humane environment - not in an inhumane and vindictive prison. To stop the future development of such personalities, we need to shift the paradigm from Haumain based institutions, to Waheguru consciousness based institutions. The consciousness evolution is not an individual effort. It is a part of the overall evolutionary process from nothingness to gasses to liquids, to solids, to plants, to animals, to human life. We are becoming more and more aware of the need to live in an interconnected spiritual consciousness. We have no choice. It is inevitable.

In our institutions, we are beginning to see the futility of war, greed, competition and exploitation. In spite of the fact that we grew up

in Haumain based institutions, we are beginning to heed the spiritual messages imparted to us by Nanaks, Christs, Baddhas and Muhammads. The punitive value judgments are also Haumain based:

Bura Bhalaa Tichar Akhada

Bad and good one says as long as there is
a sense of duality (created by Haumain)
Gurmukh recognizes the One and is merged with the One
-Sri Guru Amar Das ji

Once you recognize that the essence of all of us is the Divine within us, then we do not make value judgments. We try to understand the nature's laws and try to help the person heal himself/herself. Another person's suffering is our own.

Aval allah Noor upaia

First, Allah created Light
All humans are Nature's beings
From One Light manifest the whole universe,
Who are good, who are bad?
-Bhagat Kabir ji, SGGS - P.1349

The more we are attached to our own sense of right and wrong, the more punitive we are. These values are created by humans. A person who is too punitive toward himself is also punitive toward others. People who are punitive toward themselves are usually the ones whose parents were irrationally punitive toward them when they were children. To be kind and forgiving toward others, one has to forgive oneself first. Since Waheguru, Allah, Ram or God is merciful and forgiving, if we have a strong connection with Waheguru, we become devoid of guilt within ourselves and cease finding fault with others.

76

Who am "I"? What power do I have to be forgiving? There can be no peace in this world, as long as we glorify ourselves as individuals or nations and make punitive value judgments about other individuals and nations. There are no good and bad guys. We are all in it together. Hurt creates anger and anger creates suspicion. We live in a very paranoid civilization which is created by the hurt we caused to each other for centuries, pursuing misguided vested interest with greed and violence. We need to heal the hurt by making a concentrated effort to nurture each other, instead of continuing to hurt each other by making punitive judgments about individuals, communities and nations.

The tragic September 11, 2001 attack on the World Trade Center and the Pentagon demonstrates that the power paradigm is unworkable. Our expenditure of trillions of dollars on defense, C.I.A. and F.B.I, could not protect us. A few individuals armed with box cutters brought the world to a standstill. I shared my reaction to 9/11 tragedy in an essay "A Tragic Wake Up Call." (22) Unfortunately, we continue to use violence and power to solve human and political problems.

We need to understand the laws of nature and to nurture it with love. Punishment never makes anything grow. Physical Sciences are uncovering these Divine laws of nature. The more we understand, the more we become free of sin, guilt and punishment. There was a time when people believed that natural phenomena are a God's punishment for our sins. But we know better now - earthquakes and lightning are created according to nature's laws. The nature of our economic institutions, of organizations and the motivation of the people who run our corporations create famine and poverty. These processes can be understood and altered.

Sin, guilt, and punishment are concepts created by the power elite for control purposes, and to serve the vested interest of certain individuals or classes of individuals. This situation is totally contradictory to Divine consciousness.

Clinically, we observe that guilt creates havoc in the productive functioning of an individual. Love is the Divine principle, not violence, fear and guilt. Love brings Ananda or Bliss to the individual and the world around him or her.

Haumain creates duality. We fight for our vested interest against the "others." We do not see the reflection of the One in everyone. We dehumanize the other because of our attachment to our misconceived vested interest and ourselves, so we can murder another person and steal their assets. Rich nations continue to rob poor nations by force, or through the economic power of multi-national corporations (3,8). Leadership and the power elite in third world countries are like the Pahari Rajas (the rulers in the hill states of Punjab during Guru Gobind Singh's time, see pages 156-215), who have no interest in raising their voices against the oppressor and working toward the well being of their own people.

The nature of spiritual consciousness determines the kind of economic and political system we have. If the spiritual belief is that we are one, then, we can be our "brother's or sister's keeper." If we live in Haumain consciousness and do not see the spiritual connection with the whole universe, then we can justify plunder, murder and destruction for our own personal gain as individuals, families, clans, and nations. We may even kill other people to save their souls because of our Haumain based belief that "what I think and believe is better than what you think and believe."

Instead of trying to convince people through the use of military, economic and political power, we need to have a dialogue. One of my Muslim readers of this manuscript told me that in the Koran, Allah said, "I have created you from one man and one woman and have created many tribes so that you could have a dialogue."

Our political institutions are based on Haumain glorification, and our leaders avoid peaceful dialogue and instead use violence. Politics is a game of power manipulation. Anyone who becomes a head of state in any political system has to understand and have the skill to defeat everyone else at this game. The politicians use, and are used by, other institutions for mutual vested interest, e.g., religious, business, and academic institutions. The media also serves these institutions in order to perpetuate their vested interest. These institutions are ostensibly there to serve the people; however, because these institutions mainly run in Haumain consciousness, they create devastation and suffering. History books are filled with examples of devastation caused in the name of religious, national or ethnic economic interest. Academic institutions provide the rationalization for such devastation and create the means for such destruction. The Haumain based civilization uses the name of the spiritual beings toward Haumain satisfaction. For instance, Christ Consciousness is pure Love. Jesus prayed for the forgiveness of his murderers because they knew not what they did. He protected the adulteress who was judged by society to be a sinner. Soon after his death, the power elite began to exploit His name and started a religion based on punishment. Human beings were slaughtered like animals in the name of Christ, for personal material gains, not to serve the Creator, Its Creation, or Christ.

In the beginning of this manuscript, I outlined the Sikh Guru's concept of Creation and the purpose of the Creation. It is to realize that the Creator is the essence of all beings, to realize this consciousness within ourselves and to serve the Creator and the Creation in selfless loving consciousness. One must reduce or alleviate one's Haumain consciousness. Yet the Sikh religion has also become sectarian. Instead of bringing spiritual consciousness into political life, the Sikhs are also using religion to further their political and material gains. **Any religion that preaches sectarianism in the name of One God is furthest from God and spiritual consciousness.** Over and over, we are caught in Haumain consciousness. The tragedy is that we are not even aware of it. To live in a cosmic spiritual consciousness is not to justify that whatever is happening is God's doing, therefore, I cannot do anything and must remain in a state of inertia. In fact, if it is so willed, one is in an active state of meditation and service to the Beloved, along with keeping the company of the saints and sages that walked and still walk this planet. As we "understand" the Divine Order, we are able to detach from Haumain and duality. The achievement of such a spiritual consciousness is also not willed by an individual. It unfolds as a cosmic order; there are consequences that are not punishment based on someone's value judgment. It rains the same everywhere. Lightening strikes according to nature's laws. A tiger hunts because of its nature. If we understand its nature we can avoid being eaten. In every society we create people with different "nature." If we understand the circumstances and attitudes within a society that create certain kinds of people, we can create people who are loving, caring, and non-exploitive and bring peace and harmony to the world.

Our consciousness is evolving from inanimate to animal to human life. I don't think I willed to be evolved, or I chose to be what I am and who I am. Humans think that our intellect and technology make us superior to everyone else. **From time to time, blessed spiritual beings are manifested to remind us that we are spiritual beings, and "love" is the principle that reveals to us the spiritual and interconnected nature of this universe; the importance of the tiniest creature in this uni-**

verse. So far, human civilization is organized under Haumain principle. Now, it is becoming clearer to most people that the Haumain-based world is not workable. We have begun to see the futility of institutions created with such a consciousness. Ordinary people have access to information that exposes the hollowness of religious, business, academic and political institutions created by the Haumain-based power elite for vested interests.

The mechanisms of change are increasingly based on love and compassion instead of power. For example: the Carter Mediation Center, conflict resolution panels and conflict management training for elementary and secondary school children are among literally hundreds of grassroots organizations that are spiritually and humanistically based. The power elite is threatened by such organizations, e.g., the remarks of Dole, Buchanan and the Vatican on the Women's Summit in China, or the senior Bush's reluctance to attend the Earth Summit in Brazil. Pat Buchanan says that the International Women's Conference in Beijing was a "Crazy dingbat conference" overrun by bisexuals and homosexuals. "It was a horrible thing, dreadful. It looked like the bar scene in 'Star Wars'." President George W. Bush and his associates have a vision of an "American Century" in which they will have total global dominance. They have either withdrawn from international treaties or refused to participate. Unilateralist and "preventive strikes" have become their foreign policy. They are the judge, jury and executioner of any nation they consider to be a threat. I hope the civil society can organize under the principal of Love and Forgiveness because "they know not what they do." On the other hand, there are thousands of grassroots organizations promoting peace and justice, environmental protection and inter-faith dialogue.

We are privileged to participate in the next phase of human evolution, in which love and peace will prevail. We will be liberated from Haumain consciousness, awakened to the Source, and we will become one with It in all Its manifestations.

May we be liberated from Haumain, realize the Creator within ourselves, and use our skills and positions to serve our fellow human beings with love and selflessness.

Self Evaluation

14. PORTRAITS OF MANMUKH AND GURMUKH
The Impact of Haumain (Manmukh) and Naam Consciousness (Gurmukh) on Personal Life and Social Institutions

MANMUKH	GURMUKH
(Follows the dictates of mind)	(Follows Loving Divine Guidance)
Haumain (I am)	Naam (Divine You are)
Moh (Attachment to oneself and all one possesses)	Prem (Love of the Beloved Creator and It's Creation)
I am the cause, I am the doer	Creator causes everything and I am a part of the Divine order.
Hankaar (Pride, Hubris) I achieve, I think, I possess.	Surrender and Thankfulness. I receive gifts from the Giver.
Maya (Becoming attached to the transitory world)	Perceives Creation as a manifestation of the Creator. Remembers the Creator and enjoys it without getting attached to it.
Considers all achievements and possessions as a result of one's own efforts. Experiences mood swings dependent on personal failure or success.	Enjoys one's achievements and possessions as the gifts from the Creator and gives thanks. Minimal mood savings

MANMUKH	GURMUKH
Experiences a sense of duality	Perceives unity in diversity.
Makes punitive value judgments; good-bad, sin-virtue etc.	Manifest behavior, good-bad, sin-virtue etc. is determined by forces far beyond one's personal choice.
Believes in punishment and rewards.	Believes in Understanding the Divine order and removing the barriers that keep a person from loving and perceiving the Creator.
Exploitation of others for personal gain and glory.	Service of the Creator and Its creation
Actions motivated by personal Greed and power.	Actions motivated by Love and service
Gets caught in the cobweb of Kaam (Sexual lust), Krodh (Anger), Lobh (Greed), Moh (attachment), Hankar (Pride)	Since everything one has is a gift from the Creator, one enjoys all pleasure and human emotions without getting attached to them.
Because of a sense of Duality Discriminates against other people	At peace with everyone
Fights for personal and national Causes	Solves problems with loving consciousness
Supports war machine	Supports peaceful conflict resolution
Suspicious of others and is afraid of losing personal possessions	Trusts others and willing to share with fellow human beings
Exploits earth and its resources	Preserves environment and replenishes what he/she takes from the earth
Creates fear to control others	Neither creates fears nor is afraid

V

THE SIKH SPIRITUAL EVOLUTION

A DIVINE PLAY

VI. PRELUDE

The Historical Context: Punjab is a fertile land of the Indus Valley in the northwest India. "Punj" means five, "Aab" means water or river. This is a land of five rivers and the cradle of the Indus Valley civilization dating back to 2500 B.C. At some point in the second millennium B.C., the nomadic Aryans came to India and settled in Indus and Gangetic plains. They created Vedas that developed into Hindu religions. The capital of undivided Punjab was Lahore (now in Pakistan). It is named after Sri Ram Chandar's son Lav, and Kasoor is named after Sri Ram Chandar's son Kush. The epic Ramayana tells the story of Sri Ram Chandar, the Hindu God.

Kurukshetra in the southern Punjab (now in Haryana state of India) was the site of the greatest epic war fought between Pandavs and Kauravs described in the second great Indian epic Mahabharta. Bhagvad Gita is a part of this epic story in which Arjun, one of the Pandav brothers, the greatest archer, refused to fight and kill his Kaurav cousins. Bhagvad Gita contains 18 chapters of sermon, which Lord Krishna delivered to Arjun to convince him that as a Kashtrya warrior, it was his Dharma (the rightful duty) to fight; the outcome of life and death is not in his power.

Until Vasco de Gama discovered the sea route to India in 1498, most other travelers and conquerors came through the Khyber Pass in Afghanistan in northwest India. They had to go through Punjab to reach Delhi, the seat of political power. The Aryans came in 2000 B.C. In 327 B.C., Alexander arrived, followed by Muslim conquerors in the 8th century A.D. During Alexander's conquests from Greece to India, most countries yielded without a fight; the ones that stood in his way were defeated. The

King of Punjab, Porus, fought against Alexander and lost. Nevertheless, Alexander's army suffered heavy losses and refused to go further. On his return, Alexander gave back power to Porus and several of his officers stayed in Punjab. By the time Sri Guru Nanak Dev ji was born in 1469 A.D., Punjab had a very diverse population. Today, you can find different physical types and complexions within the same family.

By the time Guru Nanak Dev ji was born, there was a great confluence of Hindu and Islamic religions. It also led to conflicts and oppression. Sri Guru Nanak Dev ji was 56 years old when Babar, the creator of the Moghul Empire, invaded India. It is reported in the Puratan Janam Sakhi[1] (17) that Babar and Guru Nanak Dev ji met. Guru ji and his Muslim friend, Rabab player Mardana, were imprisoned along with other citizens of the town. The prisoners were given hard tasks. Guru ji continued his meditation and singing of Shabads (Songs of Divine love). News of Guru ji's imprisonment reached Babar, who came to visit him. He was so impressed by Guru ji's spiritual presence that he asked for Guru ji's blessings. Guru Nanak Dev ji told him as long as his rule was just, he would continue to rule. It is an interesting story of temporal power of the Moghuls and the Sant Sipahi (Spiritual warrior) paradigm that emerged from the succession of the ten Sikh Gurus and the embodiment of their Word in Sri Guru Granth Sahib, the holy book; the eternal Guru. The Moghul Empire was at its peak from 1525 to 1707, when Aurangzeb died. The Sikh spiritual revolution evolved from 1469 to 1708 when Sri Guru Gobind Singh ji died.

---

[1] Puratan Janam Sakhis are a biographical account of Guru Nanak Dev Ji's life.

VI. The Cast of The Divine Play: Ten Sikh Gurus and Seven Moghul Emperors

mein hoo param purkh ka daasa

I am the servant of the Perfect Being
I have come to see the world play.
                    -Sri Guru Gobind Singh ji, Bachitar Natak, P.57*

The evolution of Sikh spiritual practice over two centuries, and the simultaneous rule of the Moghul dynasty in India make a fantastic play between the spiritual pursuit of humanity with the Divine Love in heart, and the Haumain based social, political, economic and religious institutions. The play was staged in a remote part (viewed from the West) of northwest India in the Punjab State. A part of it is in Pakistan. There was an ongoing interaction between the Ten Sikh Gurus and the Moghul Emperors which provides insight into the interplay of Love for the Divine and the temptations derived from Haumain-based pursuits with Attachment (Moh) to Lust (Kaam); Anger (Krodh); Greed (Lobh) and Pride or Hubris (Hankar).

This kind of play has been staged across continents and throughout history; only the names of places and the cast were different. For examples, between Christ and the power elite at the time of the Roman Empire and Hazrat Muhammad Sahib and the power elite during his time in Mecca, Moses came to liberate the slaves from the Pharaohs.

While we participate in such a play, we do not understand its significance. Currently, we are engaged in the same play. The power elite comprised of the Haumain-based political, social, economic, academic, media and reli-

---

*Bachitar Natak is a part of Dasam Granth (21)

gious institutions, versus those striving for spiritual life and well being of the planet and Love for the Divine. **The Sikh-Moghul play might provide very important insight to each of us regarding the role we are playing in this divine play. After we realize our individual role and the** consciousness that motivates us, it may help us to let the Divine Light work through us, no matter what role we are assigned by Divine Order. The good news is, we are at the brink of the paradigm shift from Haumain based Maya to Divine Love based Reality, because we are beginning to realize that Haumain based institutions are not workable. They have brought untold suffering to humanity.

Following is the cast of characters in the divine play as it was presented on Punjabi soil.

The Sikh Gurus

1. Guru Nanak, Birthday 1469 AD.

2. Guru Angad Dev ji
3. Guru Amar Das ji
4. Guru Ramdas ji
5. Guru Arjun Dev ji
6. Guru Horgobind ji

7. Guru Har Rai ji
8. Guru Harkrishan ji
9. Guru Tegh Bahadur ji
10. Guru Gobind Singh ji
Guru Gobind Singh died
in October 1708

The Moghul Emperors

1. Emperor Babar invaded India in 1525 A.D.
2. Emperor Hamayun
3. Emperor Akbar the Great Akbar the Great
4. Emperor Jahangir Jahangir
5. Emperor ShahJahan
6. Emperor Auruangzeb Emperor Aurangzeb Emperor Aurangzeb Emperor Aurangzeb Emperor Aurangzeb died in 1707

7. Emperor Bahadur Shah

VII. A BRIEF HISTORY OF THE SIKH GURUS

1. GURU NANAK, THE SIKH
(1469-1539)

Guru Nanak Dev ji was born into Hindu Khatri family, in Talwandi village (Nankana Sahib), near Lahore, the capital of Punjab. Since the partition of India in 1947 A.D., it is in Pakistan. His father was Mehta Kalu ji and his mother was Mata Tripta ji. He had a sister Nanaki ji, and there was a legendary love between them. In Punjab, a sister and brother relationship is very unique and sacred; It is celebrated each year when the sisters tie a Rakhi (a thread or a tinseled bracelet) on the wrist of their brothers, and the brothers give gifts to their sisters. Guru Nanak Dev ji was married[1] at age 13 to Mata Sulakhni ji. She came to live with him when he was 19 years old, and had two sons, Lakshmi Chand and Siri Chand.

Guru Nanak Dev ji was very reflective right from his childhood. He was sent to study with Brahmins and Maulvis. His father wanted him to become a successful farmer or businessman but Guru ji was absorbed in the suffering of people around him. He went into the wilderness to enjoy the natural beauty and tranquility, meditate on the glories of the Creator, listen to the birds, and watch the playful animals. He expressed his experience of nature:

Balihaari kudrat vassia

Salutations to the one who resides in nature;
It is impossible to describe Your limits.
The Light is in the Form (Creation),

---

[1] Marriage in India did not have the same meaning as in the West or in modern India. The parents might get their children engaged even at birth and get them married when they were still children. But the marriage did not consummate until at the age of puberty, muklawa, when the bride began to live with the groom and his family.

And the Form is in the Light.

The Perfect Being fills the whole Universe.

Like most Punjabi village boys, he was sent to graze the cattle. He would spend his time in meditation. His father would get angry, but the Muslim village chief Rai Bular saw in the boy something very unique and spiritual in nature. He tried to persuade Guru ji's father to recognize Guru ji's spiritual devotion, but Mehta Kaluji wanted his son to grow up as a successful man.

Guru ji's father, Mehta Kalu ji, thought maybe his son would become more involved in business instead of farming. He gave him some money to go to Lahore to make a business investment.

On the way to Lahore, Guru ji saw some hungry Sadhus. He bought food and fed the Sadhus, and returned home. When his father inquired about the investment, Guru ji replied, "I have made a True Investment (Sacha Sauda)" and told what he had done. His father, like most fathers, thought his son had squandered away his money, and he slapped him. His sister Nanaki ji, rescued him from his father's beating.

Guru Nanak Dev ji spent his time visiting with the Sadhus (the holy men), who renounced this world and spent their time in devotion to the Divine. Guru ji made friends with a local Muslim musician Mardana, who played Rabab. Mardana was a Mirasi, a low caste of entertainers. Mardana stayed with Guru ji all his life and accompanied him on all his travels. Whenever Guru ji had the divine inspiration to sing the glory of Naam (Waheguru's Name), nature, devotional love or the pathos of human suffering, caught in the cobweb of Haumain pursuits; he would ask Mardana to play Rabab and Baba Nanak would sing the Shabad ("Word" emanating from Divine consciousness). Guru ji never thought the Shabads were his own creation.

jaisi mein aave khasam ki bani

How so ever the Bani (Spiritual Verses)
comes to me from the Master
O Lalo, that is the way I narrate it.
                    -Sri Gur Nanak Dev ji, SGGS - P. 722

Furthermore:

dhur ki bani aai jin sagli chint mitaai

This Bani has come from the Source
That vanquishes all worries.
                    -Sri Guru Arjan Dev ji, SGGS - P. 628

Guru ji's father continued to worry about his son's future. He was sent to Sultanpur, where his sister Bebe Nanaki's husband was employed by the Sultan. Guru ji was given the job of keeping accounts in his grocery store. For some time, he lived with his sister and brother-in-law. Later on, he set up his own residence with his wife Sulukhani and invited his friend Mardana to join him.

He saw strife between Hindus and Muslims, the ritualistic worship by Brahmins and Mullahs and the corrupt rulers. He addressed the Muslims through his Shabads. Two of them are given below:

mehar masit sidak musala hak halal Koran

Let compassion be thy mosque, Let faith be thy prayer mat,
Let honest living be thy Koran, Let modesty be the rules of obser-
    vance,
Let piety be the fasts you keep;
In such ways strive to become a Muslim:
Right conduct the Ka'ba; Truth the Prophet, Good deeds thy prayer;
Submission to the Divine Will thy rosary;
Nanak, if this you do, the Divine will be your Protector. (25)
                    -Sri Guru Nanak Dev ji, SGGS. P.140

panj nivajan vakht panj

Five prayers, five times a day
With five different names;
Make the first prayer, truth,
The second to lawfully earn your daily bread;
The third: charity in the name of God;
 Fourth; purity of mind,
Fifth: the adoration of Divine
Practice these five virtues,
And let good deeds be your article of faith: the Kalama;
Then you can call yourself truly a Muslim.
By the practice of hypocrisy,
Nanak, a man is deemed false through and through. (25)
                    -Sri Guru Nanak Dev ji, SGGS - P.141

He addressed the people absorbed in worldly pursuits.

kia khadai kia paidhai hoe

What is the use of rich food and fine clothes?
When the Truth does not dwell within us?
What is the use of fresh fruit, of sugar, of butter?
Of flour and meat in abundance,
Of splendid raiment's, and of soft beds,
And a life of sensual delight?
What use to a king his armies,
His wise ministers and his brave commanders?
If in his heart he has not the Divine Naam.
Nanak, all these things are as dust. (25)
                    -Sri Guru Nanak Dev ji, SGGS - P.142

Guru ji described the rulers of the time.

kal kati raje kasai dharam pankh kar udaria

This age is like a drawn sword,
The kings are butchers;

Goodness hath taken wings and flown.
In the dark night of falsehood.
I espy not the moon of Truth anywhere;
I grope after Truth and am bewildered.
I see no path in the darkness;
It is the obstinacy with which
Man clings to his petty Haumain
That causes this anguish.
Nanak asks: where is the path of salvation? (25)

-Sri Guru Nanak Dev ji, SGGS - P. 145

Guru ji defined the Brahmin:

A true Brahmin is one who grasps Brahma.
Meditation on Divine and self-control are his daily routine;
His religious observances are right conduct
And an unfretting heart
He removes the lustful chains that bind the soul.
Such a Brahmin deserves all praise and honor.

-Sri Guru Nanak Dev ji, Sloak Vadhik

The Brahmins would give a sacred thread to the Hindus. Guru ji refused to wear this thread and addressed the Brahmin:

daya kapah santokh sut

Of the cotton of compassion,
Spin the thread of contentment,
Tie the knot of continence,
Give it the twist of virtues;
Make such a sacred thread
O Pundit, for your inner self.
Such a thread will not break,
Nor get soiled, be burnt, be lost.
Blessed is the man, O Nanak,
Who makes it a part of his life.

This cotton thread, for a penny you buy
Sitting in a square, mud plastered,
You put it around the necks of others.
In the ears some words you whisper, O Brahmin,
And claim to be a spiritual teacher.

With the death of the wearer falls the thread,
Thus without the thread he departs from the earth. (25)
-Sri Guru Nanak Dev ji, SGGS - P.471

He defined the Dharma of a Kshtari:

A true Kashtri, of the warrior caste,
One whose valor shows itself in every detail of his life.
The aim of his life is loving kindness,
Which he gives to the deserving,
And so becomes acceptable to .
Any man who moved by greed, preaches falsehood,
In the end must pay the penalty for his deeds. (25)
-Sri Guru Nanak Dev ji, SloakVakhik

Guru ji saw women being disrespected and wrote against it:

bhand jamiai bhand nimiai

Of a woman are we conceived,
Of a woman are we born,
To a woman are we betrothed and married.
It is a woman who is a friend and partner of life,
It is a woman who keeps the race going,
Another companion is sought when the life-partner dies,
Through a woman are established social ties.
Why should we consider woman cursed and condemned
When from woman are born leaders and rulers.
From woman alone is born a woman,
Without a woman there can be no human birth.
Without woman, O Nanak, only the True One exists.

Be it men or be it women,
Only those who sing Its glory
Are blessed and radiant with Its Beauty,
In Its Presence and with Its grace
They appear with a radiant face. (25)

Guru Nanak and Mardana would do Kirtan i.e., sing Gurbani as revealed to Guru Nanak Dev ji and Mardana would play Rabab. People would gather to hear them sing. His beautiful and peace-giving Gurbani became a household recitation in Punjab.

One day, Guru ji went to the river Bein outside of Sultanpur, and did not return. People looked for him. They found his clothes by the river but no trace of him. After three days, he re-appeared. People tried to ask him, where did he go? What happened to him? He did not answer anyone but uttered,

"There is no Hindu no Musalman." (17, P.43)

Also Guru Arjan Dev ji wrote,

Na hum Hindu na Musalman

I am neither Hindu nor a Muslim
-Sri Guru Arjan Dev ji, SGGS - P.1136

Soon after, Guru Nanak Dev ji took four journeys. In the West, he went to Mecca and Bagdad. In the East, he went to Assam. In the South, he went to Ceylon (Sri Lanka), and in the North, he went up to Tibet.

Guru Nanak, The Sikh

Guru ji realized the Eternal Creator within himself. The creator was his Guru and Nanak was his Sikh.

" Guru, the First Principle,
The Pure one is in all things
Of this there is no doubt,
Nanak has obtained the Creator,
The Infinite Supreme Being as his Guru."

Guru ji narrated his search:

gurmukh khojat bhae udasi

Gurmukh left his home to look for a saint;
The desire to see the Beloved
Had made him a hermit.
My trade is in truth,
Through the grace of Guru
I shall set free my companions. (25)

- Sri Guru Nanak Dev ji, SGGS - P.939

Waheguru gave Sri Guru Nanak Dev ji employment, which he described
in the following Shabad:

haun dhadhi vekar kare lay

I was a minstrel out of work;
The lord gave me employment.
The Mighty One instructed me:
Night and day, sing my praise!
The Lord did summon this minstrel
To his High Court*;
On me He bestowed the robe of honor
Of those who exalt Him
On me He bestowed the Nectar in a Cup,
The Nectar of His True and Holy Naam
Those who at the bidding of the Guru
Feast and take their fill

---

*The Sikhs believe when Guru Nanak disappeared in the river Bein, he was
summoned to have an audience with the Divine.

98

Of the Lord's Holiness
Attain peace and joy. (25)

-Sri Guru Nanak Dev ji, SGGS - P. 150

Naam became inseparable from Guru ji's life breath.

je dehi dukh laiaia pap gareh do rah

Though my body be crippled with disease,
Though the relentless stars bring endless misfortune on me,
Though bloody tyrants fill my soul with terror,
Though all these miseries be at once heaped on my head,
Even then, my Beloved, I shall praise You;
And I shall not grow weary of
Exalting Your Holy Naam. (25)

-Sri Guru Nanak Dev ji, SGGS - P.142

The love of Waheguru became the eternal joy.

re man aisi har sion preet kar

Listen my heart!
Let your love be that of the lotus for the pond,
Though the ripples shake the lotus and torment it,
It flowers and loves even more the waters.
Let your love be that of a fish for the water
Without which they perish.
O my heart how shall you find freedom
Except to find it through love
In the hearts of His saints
The Divine dwells
To them It gives the treasure of true devotion.

Listen, my heart: love Divine ceaselessly
As the fish loves water:
The deeper the water
The happier and more tranquil the fish
Creator alone knows the suffering
Of a fish separated from the waters.

O my heart, listen:
Love Creator as the Chatrik bird loves the raindrops
Rivers in spate and the drenched uplands
Are of no avail to the Chatrik;
Nothing but the raindrops can quench its thirst.
As a man sows, so shall he reap.
That which the Creator ordains must come to pass.

O my heart, listen
Love Divine as water loves milk.
The water must suffer, must evaporate
Before the heat can touch the milk.
Creator is the Separator,
Creator is the Joiner.
The Divine is that which exalts through Truth.

O my heart listen:
Love Divine as the Sheldrake in the fable loves the sun;
It slept not for a moment:
At night when it cannot see,
It considers the Beloved, who is close to being far,
The Haumain driven are involved in calculations,
But what the Creator ordains comes to pass.
And how so ever hard a man endeavors,
Who can tell of His Bounds?
Only through the Guru's teaching is this revealed;
In Truth alone is our peace.

Those who encounter the Guru
Achieve an indestructible love of Divine.
The Guru bestows Divine Knowledge
And unveils the mysteries of the three worlds.
That man whose feet are set
On the path of virtue
Never abandons the pure Naam.

Gone are those free birds of the air,
Who had their nurture on the happy plaines.

How transient is life?
All its sport but the fleeting joy of a moment
Who is very successful?
Who wins any game?
Except by the Will of the Creator?
Without the Guru's help we cannot burn
To nothingness the ashes of self-love; (Haumain)
For the Guru kindles in the human hearts
The Fire of the love of Naam
Through the Guru's Word alone
There comes the moment of knowing:
'My self is that Self
Through faith in the Guru the True Self is known.
What else do we need to know?

The self is ever one with the Self:
This certainty is obtained through the Guru's Word.
But those who are tied to their Haumain
Shall not know this.
Separation and frustrations are their lot.
Nanak, Naam is the one Way,
Naam is the one goal;
There is no other refuge. (25)

-Sri Guru Nanak Dev ji, SGGS - P.59-60

Through loving devotion and Naam Simran Guru Nanak Dev ji discovered that Haumain is the worst kind of disease (See pages 55-65). By the grace of Waheguru one can alleviate Haumain through Naam Simran. In the first Pauri of Japji Sahib, Guru Nanak Dev ji raises the question, how can we break down the wall of falsehood from our consciousness and remove this darkness?

sochai soch na hova-I je sochi lakhvar

The purity of mind cannot be achieved even
if the body is washed a hundred thousand times;
Nor by outer silence and long deep meditation

Can the inner silence be reached.
Nor is man's hunger appeasable
By piling up world-loads of wealth.
All the innumerable devices of worldly wisdom
Leave a man disappointed, not one avails.

How then shall we know the Truth?
How shall we rend the veils of false illusion?
Abide by the Divine Order and Its Will
O Nanak, that came inscribed within you.
-Sri Guru Nanak Dev ji, SGGS - P. 1

Guru ji concluded, by recognizing the Divine Order and surrender to the Will of the Creator which is etched in our consciousness, one can re-move the veil of falsehood and recognize the Reality, the Divine Source. He continues in the second Pauri.

Through Its Divine Order all forms are created.
It is hard to describe the Divine Order.
Greatness is received through Its order.
Through Its orders are created low and high.
It is through Its orders we receive suffering and comfort.
Through Its orders some are blessed,
And others are caught in a cycle (Of birth and death).
Everything is in Divine Order
Nothing is outside of it.
Nanak says, if one understands the Divine order,
Then one does not make Haumain claims.
(That I am the doer or I am the cause)
-Sri Guru Nanak Dev ji, SGGS - P. 1

There are 958 Sahbads by Guru Nanak Dev ji in Sri Guru Granth Sahib. There are volumes written about the stories of his encounters during his travels. I have quoted only a few of his Shabads and I may narrate a few of the stories as an introduction.

Guru Nanak Dev ji felt that one does not have to renounce the world to realize Waheguru. On the contrary, he felt that one should live in this world, but with Waheguru consciousness; that is, to live the life of a Gurmukh, the one whose face (consciousness) is always turned toward Waheguru. A Gurmukh recognizes the Divine order and relinquishes his/her Haumain. A Manmukh is the one whose consciousness is attached to his Haumain and is guided by Haumain consciousness. Living the life of a householder with Waheguru consciousness is considered the greatest spiritual attainment. One should preserve and enjoy Waheguru's creation and gifts. One can be liberated from suffering while laughing, playing, eating and dressing up. Only avoid that eating which creates disease in body and evil thoughts in the mind.

Nanak satgur bhatea

Nanak, serving the True Guru (the Creator) it is revealed
Laughing, playing, dressing up and eating one can be emancipated.
-Sri Guru Arjan Dev ji, SGGS - P.522

During Guru ji's travels, he came across a Sidha Ashram of Charpat Yogi. The Yogis who had renounced the world asked Guru ji, how can he teach that one can live like a householder in this world because the worldly Karma is so powerful that one can never sustain spiritual life. To demonstrate his point, the Yogi took a piece of paper and put it in the water. Of course, the paper could not sustain its texture and became mildewed. Guru Nanak Dev ji asked that the mustard oil lamp be brought to him. He dipped the paper in the mustard oil and put it in the water. The water did not have an impact on it. Guru ji explained, as the protective layer of oil prevents the effect of water on the paper, so love of Naam protects the householder from the impact of worldly Karma. Guru ji's encounter with Sidhas is written in Sidh Ghosht (conversation with the Sidhas). Some excerpts are given below.

Charpat Yogi questions:

> The sea of life is hard to cross,
> How can we safely reach the other shore?

Guru ji answers,

> *ape akhai ape samjhai*

> You have stated the problem correctly,
> What answer then, need I give you?
> As the lotus flower does not drown in the pool,
> As the duck is not made wet by the pond.
> As the flower thrusts upwards,
> As the duck swims,
> So with the mind intent
> Upon the Word of the Guru
> One can safely cross
> The great sea of life,
> Repeating the Holy Naam,
> Living in an aloneness
> Utterly intent, upon the One.
> In a life of worldly hopes,
> Purging the mind of worldly desires
> Nanak is the slave of the one who grasps the ungraspable
> And makes others grasp Him.

Yogi asked:

> What is the source of your knowledge?
> To what period belongs your system?
> Who is your Guru, and who are your disciples?
> What teaching keeps you in detachment?
> Tell us all this, my Child?

Guru Nanak answered:

> *pavan arambh satgur mat vela*

> With the beginning of the breath of life,
> My system began also.

Its source is the Wisdom of the True Guru,
The True Guru is the Word,
And the human mind is the disciple.
What keeps me in my detachment?
Is meditating on the Ungraspable One,
Through the One Divine word
Creator is made real to us,
And the saints destroy the flames of Haumain attachment.

Yogi asked:

Main ke dant kion khaiai sar

How can steel be chewed with waxen teeth?
What drug can cure the disease of pride?
How shall we dress a snowman in fire?
In what cage can the mind rest in peace?
What is it that is everywhere?
With which every mind should be one?
What object of concentration
Can teach the mind to turn wholly to Itself?

Guru Nanak answered:

haun haun mai main vico

From within, from within,
Make the self as nothing as nothing
Root out all feelings of otherness
And become at one with the Creator.
True the world is as hard as Steel
For the stubborn and the self-willed,
But through the might of Waheguru
This steel can be digested.
Outside yourself and within yourself
Seek only knowledge of the Creator.
By the blessings of the True Guru
The flames of desires can be destroyed. (25)
                    -Sri Guru Nanak Dev ji, SGGS - P. 938-943

In Guru ji's travels, he came across thugs, cannibals, cruel and greedy feudal lords, rich businessmen and fanatic religious zealots. **They were not evil people. They had forgotten Waheguru because of the intensity of their involvement in Haumain based pursuits. Since the divine light reflected through Guru Nanak Dev ji, they remembered their True Self and relinquished their suffering. There are no good or bad people. It is only through our forgetfulness of our True Source that we cause suffering to ourselves and others through our Haumain-based Karma.**

Bura bhala tichar akhda

One says good and bad only as long as one has a sense of duality.
Gurmukh has realized One and has merged in the One.

-SGGS - P.757

Haumain causes the sense of duality. Guru Nanak Dev ji did not make a judgment about people. His presence enabled them to get in touch with their True Self and lifted the veil of Haumain darkness. Following are but a few encounters during his vast travels.

There was a thug named Sheikh Sajjan. He built an Inn for travelers. He had a mosque for the Muslims to pray in, and a temple for the Hindus to do Pooja. He entertained and fed his guests lavishly. At night, he would kill them and rob them of all their possessions. Guru Nanak Dev ji and his companion Mardana ji stopped at his Inn. After meals, Sajjan beseeched them to go to bed, because they must be tired. Guru Nanak Dev ji said that he had to do his evening recitatation and Kirtan. In addition to his usual evening recitation, he sang the following Shabad in Raag Soohi, in which he described the hypocritical facade of people who pretend to be saints, but actually prey on the innocence of others. Without Naam, all the wealth and palaces are to no avail.

Bright sparkles the bronze;
Rub it and its soil comes off,
Wash it as much as one may
But its inner impurities go not.

Those are the friends who accompany you
When you depart from this earth.
When Dharam Raj asks for you
To account for your life,
They stand by you.
All these great edifices and palaces you are attached to
They crumble down and are useless.
They are hollow inside.

The heron is robed in white
And abides he on a pilgrim station,
But he ruthlessly devours creatures.
How can his whiteness proclaim his purity?
My body is like a Simmal tree
People are taken in by my vain majesty
But as are its fruits useless
So is my body without virtue.

Blindman carrying a load
On a very difficult road cannot see.
How can he reach his destination?
Any other service, goodness and wisdom are of no avail
Nanak, gather the wealth of Naam,
It will free you from your bondage.
                    -Sri Guru Nanak Dev ji, SGGS - P. 729

Listening to this Shabad, Sajjan was awakened. He gave up his cruel ways and established a true Dharamsala (a free inn, which every village in Punjab has for travelers) and served his fellow human beings for the rest of his life.

Once, Guru ji was passing through the village of a feudal lord named Malik Bhago. Guru Nanak stayed with a poor carpenter Bhai Lalo. Malik Bhago had arranged a big feast for all the Sadhus, faqirs and holy men for their blessings. Everyone went to his feast, but Guru ji stayed back with the poor carpenter Bhai Lalo. When Malik Bhago found out about this, he sent for Guru ji and asked him why he did not come to the feast. It is said that Guru Nanak Dev ji took Malik Bhago's gourmet food in one hand, and Bhai Lalo's simple bread in another hand. When he squeezed them blood dripped out of the rich gourmet food and milk dripped out of the simple bread of Bhai Lalo. Guru ji wanted to impress upon Malik Bhago that riches and wealth accumulated by the hard labor of poor people is like squeezing blood out of the poor working class. The simple bread of Bhai Lalo was the result of his honest labor. Bhai Lalo served Guru ji out of love and devotion. He did not want any material blessings as people like Malik Bhago do, when they invite the so-called holy men to give their blessings for more material gains.

When Guru ji was traveling in the northeast of India, Mardana became hungry. Guru ji sent him to get some food. On his way, Kauda Rakshas, the cannibal, caught him. After a while, Guru ji went to look for him. He arrived at Kauda Rakhshis's place, where Kauda was heating the oil in a big cauldron to fry Mardana ji. Guru Nanak Dev ji's presence cooled his soul. He also realized his True Self, and became a Waheguru loving person.

When Guru ji arrived in Mecca and laid down to rest, the local Mullah saw him lying and got infuriated because he saw that Guru ji was lying with his feet toward Kabah. He came to Guru ji and roared, why was Guru ji so disrespectful so as to have his feet toward the house of Allah*.

---

*Dr. Rahmany wrote, "The Holy Quoran says, to every side you turn, there is Allah."

Guru ji said that he was a tired old man, and asked if he could just move his feet in the direction where there was no Allah. It is said that no matter what direction he moved Guru ji's feet, he saw Kabah. He realized that Allah is everywhere. Most of all, it is within us. The Mullah realized that he was in the presence of a person, who had realized Allah within himself, and that the Light manifested through him. The Imam of Mecca honored him and gave him a robe with writings from Quoran-Sharif.

When Guru Nanak Dev ji reached Jagan Nath Puri, he saw that in the evening, the Brahmin started singing the Arti (salutation) in front of the statue of Jagan Nath. He had oil lamps and incense in a platter and circled around them in front of the statue. Guru ji did not participate. When the Brahmin asked him why he did not sing along, Guru ji sang the following Shabad that described the whole universe in a state of awe and wonder. Experiencing the beauty of this universe is the true Arti (Salutation) to the Creator.

gagan mai thaal ravi chand dipak banai

The sky is Your Platter,
The sun and the moon your lights;
The stars are as pearls scattered,
The woods of sandal are your incense.
The breezes blow your royal fan;
The flowers of the forests,
Lie as offerings at your feet.
What wonderful a worship with lamps is this
O You destroyer of fear!
Unstruck Music is the sound of your temple drums.
Thousands are your eyes,
And yet you have no eyes.
Thousands are your shapes,
And yet you have no shape.
Thousands are your pure feet.

And yet you have not one foot.
Thousands are your noses
And yet you have no nose.
All this is your play that enchants me.
In every heart there is light.
That light is you.
By the Light that is of Guru Himself
Is every soul illumined
But this divine Light becomes manifest
Only by the Guru's grace
What is pleasing to you, O Waheguru
Is the best Arti (worship with oil lamps in a platter)

O Guru, my mind yearns for your lotus feet,
As the honeybee for the nectar of the flowers
Night and day I thirst for you,
Give water of your mercy to Nanak:
He is like the Sarang that drinks only raindrops
So that he may dwell ever in peace of your Naam (25).
-Sri Guru Nanak Dev ji, SGGS - P. 13

The above Shabad is a part of the evening recitation meditation of a Sikh.

After the first two journeys from Sultanpur in 1500 A.D. and 1506 A.D. to 1509 A.D., Guru Nanak Dev ji settled in Kartarpur with his family. He took two journeys, from Kartarpur in 1514 A.D. to 1516 A.D. and 1518 A.D to 1521 A.D. From 1521 to 1539, he lived there as a farmer. Guru Nanak, the Sikh, would awaken three hours before dawn to meditate on Naam and recite Jap ji Sahib. At dawn, he would do Kirtan of Asa Di Var with the accompaniment of Mardana ji. At the end of the Kirtan, everybody received the blessed food, Karrah Parsad (wheat pudding). Other people began to light up through Gursikh consciousness. They would come to join Guru ji and Mardana ji's Kirtan and Gurbani recitation. In the evening, they would recite Rehras (Salutation) comprised of Sodar and Sopurkh Banis. The people who awakened to Waheguru consciousness would observe the following routine, whether or not they could visit Guru ji.

Get up two to three hours before dawn and Meditate on Naam and recite Jap ji Sahib.

At Dawn: Asa Di Var Kirtan
After the day's work, at sunset recite Rehras sahib Paath (Recitation Meditation).

Before going to sleep: Kirtan Sohila paath.

In 1539 Guru Nanak Dev ji passed on the Guruship to Bhai Lehna ji and called him Angad (Flesh of his Flesh). A brief description of his life is given in the next chapter.

When Guru ji was going to Joty Jot Sma (the light merges with the Light i.e., departure of soul from this body), the Sikhs gathered around him. Guru Nanak Dev ji was called:

> *Nanak shah faqir,*
> *hindu ka guru and muslim ka pir.*

Nanak Shah Faqir is the Guru of the Hindus and Pir of the Muslims

Both Hindus and Muslims became his followers. Ironically, at the moment of his departure from his body, the Muslims and Hindus started arguing about the last rites for his body. In their Haumain consciousness, they forgot the true spirit and got caught in formal rituals. The Muslims wanted to bury him, and the Hindus wanted to cremate him. Some wise men told them that each of these communities should keep flowers on each side of his body. The community whose flowers remained fresh until the morning will take the body and dispose of it according to its rites. In the morning when people came, there was no body but the flowers on both sides were fresh. The Hindus cremated the flowers and the Muslims buried the flowers.

salahi salah eti surt na paiai

> Thy praisers praise Thee,
> And know not Thy greatness
> As rivers and streams flow into the sea,
> But know not its vastness (25)

Summary

Guru Nanak created a spiritual consciousness of loving devotion to Waheguru and Its Creation. It is beyond human endeavour to understand the Divine Order. Everything is in Divine Order and we are a part of it. If one understands that, then one does not make Haumain based claims, accepts the Creator's Will and does not make punitive value judgments on a person's lot in life. He raised the level of social consciousness to the extent that people began to realize the futility of ritualistic and hypocritical religious practices. He brought unity to a diverse Punjab population and raised his loving voice against any kind of discrimination based on caste, religion or gender, etc. He created Waheguru consciousness in the rich and ruling class exploiters and criminal elements, and they began to serve their fellow human beings.

Sri Guru Nanak Dev ji and Emperor Babar

During his travels, Guru Nanak Dev ji passed through Sayidpur and visited his friend Lalo. People complained that under Ibrahim Lodhi's rule, people were subjected to oppression and unjust treatment. Guru Sahib responded that a great calamity was about to befall on the city. He asked Mardana to play the Rabab and he sang the following Shabad describing the agony as a result of the greed and ambitions of Babar, and the demoralization of Hindustan (India).

jaisi mein aveh khasam ki bani

As the word of the Divine descends upon me,
So I make it known, my friend Lallo.
With evil as his best man,
Bringing a crowd of misdeeds as his bridal procession.
Like a bridegroom Babar has hastened from Kabul,
To seize by force as his bride, O Lallo,
The wealth of Hindustan.
Modesty and righteousness have both vanished away,
Falsehood leading the van holds the field, O Lallo,
Both the Qazi and the Brahmin are out of work.
The devil reads the marriage services.
Muslim women who read the Koran,
In their agony will cry Allah, O Lallo!
Hindu women of high caste or low caste
Will meet the same dire fate.
Men will sing hymn in praise of murder, O Nanak,
And instead of saffron smear themselves with blood.
Though this is a city of corpses, Nanak exalts the creator in it,
And utters this true saying.
The Divine who made men,
Gave them their different stations:
He sits aloof from their doings and watches them all. (11)
-Sri Guru Nanak Dev ji, SGGS, P722-23

Guru Nanak Dev ji described the painful scene, how the women who lived in luxurious palaces and were waited on by maids, were dishonored and humiliated in public during Babar's invasion.

jin sir sohan pattian maangi pae sandhur

They who wore beautiful tresses
And the partings of whose hair were dyed with vermilion,
Have their locks now shorn with scissors,
And dust is thrown upon their heads.
They dwelt in their private chambers;

Now they cannot find a seat in public.
Hail the Creator
O Primal Being, Your limit is not known.
You make and behold the
Different phases of existence.
When they were married,
They appeared beautiful near their spouses.
They came in their sedans adorned with ivory.
Water was waved round their heads
And glittering fans over them.
And hundreds of thousands waiting on them..
Eating coconuts and dates they sported on their couches.
But now chains are on their necks,
and broken are their strings of pearls;
The wealth and beauty that gave them pleasure
Have become their bane.
The order was given to the soldiers to take and dishonor them.
If it pleases the Creator, He gives greatness, and if it please Him,
 Gives punishment.
If they had thought of Him before,
Why should they have received punishment?
But they had lost all thought of the Creator in joys,
In spectacles and in pleasures.
When Babar's rule was proclaimed
No Pathan prince ate his food.
How shall Hindu women now bathe and apply frontal marks
Without their sacred squares?
They who never thought of Ram
Are not now allowed even to mention Khuda.
One may return to her home
Another may meet and inquire after the safety of a relation.
But others are destined to sit and weep in pain.
What pleases the Creator, O Nanak, shall happen. What is man?
                              -Sri Guru Nanak Dev ji, SGGS - P. 417

Seeing the pain and misery caused by Babar's invasion Guru Nanak cried out to Waheguru; "Didn't he feel any pain?" and answered himself in the following Shabad.

Babar ruled over Khurasan and had terrified Hindustan
The Creator takes no blame to Himself,
It was Death disguised as a Mohgul who made war on Hindustan.
When there was such slaughter and lamentation,
Did not you, O Creator, feel pain?
Creator, you belong to all.
If a tyrant slay a tyrant, one is not angry;
But if a ravening lion falls on a herd,
Its master should show his manliness.
The dogs of Lodi have spoiled the priceless inheritance;
When they are dead no one will regard them.
O Creator, you yourself join and you yourself separate
Lo! This is your greatness.
If any one gives oneself a great name
And enjoys himself to his heart's content,
In Creator's view he is as a worm that nibbles corn;
But he who is dead while alive, may gain something,
O Nanak, by meditating on Naam.

By "dead" in the above line, Guru Sahib means the one who has relinquished his/her Haumain attachment.

Guru Sahib and Mardana were imprisoned with other citizens and given hard labor. Guru Sahib continued his Simran and sang Shabads deploring the painful conditions of the prisoners and exalting Waheguru.

Babar was informed of this Faqir Baba Nanak. Babar visited Guru Sahib in prison and they discussed religious matters. He realized that he was in the presence of a spiritual being. Generally, the Muslim rulers had a great respect for Faqirs. He asked Guru Sahib for his blessings. Guru Sahib said to him:

"Deliver just judgments, revere holy men, forswear wine and gambling. The Monarch who indulges in these vices, if he survives, bewails of his misdeeds. Be merciful to the vanquished and worship God in spirit and in Truth" (11)

2. SIRI GURU ANGAD DEV JI
(1504 – 1552.)

Sri Guru Nanak Dev ji passed the Divine Light on to Sri Guru Angad Dev ji. Sri Guru Nanak Dev ji had been the Sikh of the Divine Waheguru and served with intense passion and loving devotion until he was nothing but Divine Light. Whoever came into his presence also realized their True Identity and was lit up with the same Divine Light.

Guru Angad Dev ji's name was Bhai Lehna. He was born on March 31, 1504 at Harike in Ferozepur district. His father, Pheru, owned a small business. He moved to Khadur in Distt, Amritsar, after the invasion of Babar and was a devotee of Jawala Mukhi Temple of the goddess Durga in Kangra Distt. One day, he happened to hear Bhai Jodha singing Guru Nanak's Bani. He decided to visit Guru Nanak Dev ji while on his way to Jawala Mukhi temple in the Kangra Hills..

When Bhai Lehna ji reached near Kartarpur, he asked an old man if he knew where Guru Nanak lived. The man told him to follow him. While the man walked ahead of him, Bhai Lehna ji followed on his horse. When they arrived at the house the man told him that he could come in the house with him. When Bhai Lehna realized that it was Guru Nanak Dev ji, the old man coming from his fields who led him on foot while he rode his horse, he was impressed by Guru Nanak Dev ji's humility and simplicity.

Bhai Lehna ji decided to stay and serve Guru ji, and he never left. While Guru Nanak loved and served the Divine, which most people could not see, Bhai Lehna ji set an example of how to serve the Divine in the human form of Guru Nanak Dev ji. He served Guru ji with tireless devotion. Once, Bhai Lehna ji visited Guru ji wearing new clothes. Guru ji was in the fields getting fodder for the cattle. It had rained and the fields were quite muddy, and so were the bundles of cattle feed. Guru Nanak Dev ji's son did not want to get muddy and wet, but Bhai Lehna ji volunteered to carry the bundles home.

When they reached home, Guru ji's wife Mata Sulukhani ji was quite upset that Guru ji had not treated his guest, Bhai Lehna ji well. All his new clothes were soiled. Guru ji replied that it was not dirt on his clothes, but saffron used on ceremonial occasions. There is a Punjabi folklore that describes the importance of selfless service:

sewa nu milda mewa, kar ke koi dekh lao

Sewa (Selfless Service) bears fruit,
Let anyone do it and see for himself.

After Bhai Lehna ji became the Guru he wrote beautiful poetry about loving service to the Divine Guru:

eh kinehi ashki Doojhe lagge jai

What kind of Love is this that shifts to someone else?
Those are true lovers, who are forever merged with the Beloved.

changeh changa kar manai

If one responds to good by being good
Responds to bad by being bad
Those are not the lovers
Who act in such a business like manner.

117

Loving is an unconditional acceptance and devotion:

salaam jabaab doven kareh

If one argues with the Beloved
Such a person is lost from the beginning.

There are numerous stories of Bhai Lehna's devotion and service to Guru Nanak Dev ji. When Guru ji decided to pass on the Light, he created a very strange appearance by wearing rags that were torn and dirty, as if he had gone mad, admonishing people to leave him as he headed toward the forest. Some people thought he had gone mad and they went their own merry way. Others continued following him. He took a pouch of gold coins and showered the gold coins at them. They felt satisfied and also left him. Ultimately, only Bhai Lehna still followed him. When they reached the thick of the forest, they saw a corpse covered with a white sheet. Guru ji asked Bhai Lehna ji to eat the corpse. Bhai lehna ji asked if he should start eating from the feet or the head. When he removed the white sheet, there was *Karrah prasad* (wheat pudding) instead of a corpse.

Guru ji returned home and prepared for the ceremony to declare Bhai Lehna ji as the Guru and called him Angad, signifying the complete merger of the Sikh with the Guru.

Guru Angad Dev ji continued the awakening of people from the slumber of Haumain based pursuits. In addition, he further developed the Gurmukhi script. There are unique sounds in the Punjabi language and the Gurmukhi script is well suited for it. For the most part if you can speak Punjabi, you can write it; if you can read it, you can pronounce the words correctly because each consonant and vowel connotes only one sound. Guru Angad Dev ji also had two Muslim musicians Sata and Balwand to do Kirtan for the Sangat. They continued to serve the Guru and the Sangat until the fifth Guru Arjan Dev ji.

118

Guru Angad Dev ji was interested in educating people, and he started formal education. He was especially interested in the education of children and used to teach children himself.

Moghul Emperor Humayun's Visit

Instead of anointing either of his two sons, Baba Sri Chand and Laxmi Chand as the Guru, Guru Nanak Dev ji passed on the Divine Light to Guru Angad Dev ji because of his ability to incorporate the Loving Devotion to the Divine, although Baba Sri Chand was a very spiritual person, he founded an ascetical sect called Udasi. The Udasis renounce the householder's responsibilities.

Around this time, the founder of the Moghul Empire, Babar, passed on his empire to his son Humayun. Sher Shah Suri challenged him and defeated him in both battles of Panipat. Humayun escaped to Lahore in the Punjab and visited Guru Nanak Dev ji's successor Guru Angad Dev ji and went to visit him in Khadur Sahib. Guru ji was in deep meditation and did not pay attention to Humayun's arrival, which enraged Humayun. He was ready to take out his sword to punish the Guru ji for his apparent disregard, when Guru ji opened his eyes and said he should have used his sword in Panipat against Sher Shah Suri. It would not accomplish anything using a sword against a God loving Faqir. Humayon felt a sense of peace in Guru ji's presence and asked for his blessings. Guru ji repeated Guru Nanak's blessings i.e. as long as he would rule justly and compassionately, he would continue to rule. He should regroup his armies to succeed in regaining his throne, and he did. Sri Guru Granth Sahib contains 63 of Sri Guru Angad Dev ji's poetical compositions.

Guru Angad Dev ji passed on the Light to the third Guru Amar Das ji.

3. SRI GURU AMAR DAS JI
(1479 - 1574.)

Guru Amar Das ji was born in Basarke in the Amritsar district on May 5, 1479. His father was Tej Bhan, and his mother was Bakht Kaur. His nephew was married to Guru Angad Dev ji's daughter Bibi Amro. One day, he heard her sing Guru Nanak's Bani and he was moved by the sweet devotional and inspiring quality of the verses. He asked his niece- in- law where she learned the verses. When she told him that she learned them from her father Guru Angad Dev ji, Bhai Amar Das decided to visit Sri Guru Angad Dev ji. At this time, he was 20 years older than Guru Angad Dev ji. When he reached Khadur Sahib, Guru Angad Dev ji greeted him. He wanted to bow down and touch his feet because Bhai Amar Das was an elder, being the uncle- in- law of his daughter. Bhai Amar Das stopped Guru ji. Instead, he bowed down to Guru ji and touched his feet, saying he had not come to him as a relative. He decided to be his Sikh.

Bhai Amar Das ji's devotion and service was legendary. He would carry pitchers of water from the river early in the morning for Guru ji's bath. He would spend most of his time in doing service in Langar, or doing chores for Guru Ghar (house). When the time came for Guru Angad Dev ji to pass on the Light, he chose Bhai Amar Das over his son Datu.

Datu was quite enraged. Being the son of the Guru, he thought he should have succeeded as the Guru. He went to Guru Amar Das. He kicked him down from his seat, saying that Guru Amar Das was just a servant of his father. Guru ji caressed his feet and said, " My bones are old, I hope they did not hurt your tender feet".

Guru Amar Das ji left Khadur Sahib and returned to his village Basarke. The Sikhs never recognized Datu as the Guru, the Sikhs went to Baba

Budha ji. His name is one of the most important in the story of the Gurus. He was the most respected Sikh who lived from Guru Nanak's time, to the time of the sixth Guru Sri Guru Hargobind Sahib. He witnessed and performed the ceremony of transferring the responsibilities of Guruship for the five Gurus. Bhai Budha ji lived in Pipli Sahib, Amritsar. The Sikhs told him that Guru Amar Das ji left Khadur Sahib because Guru Angad Dev ji's son, Datu, laid claim to the Guruship. Since the Sikhs did not recognize him, he loaded all his possessions on a camel and left. On the way, he was robbed by the bandits. The Sikhs asked Baba Budha ji to plead with Guru Amar Das ji to come back and take over the responsibilities of Guruship. Baba Budha ji led the Sikhs to Basarke and pleaded with Guru Amar Das ji to provide spiritual guidance to the Sikhs.

Guru Amar Das ji reappeared and continued serving the Sikhs for 22 years. In addition to spiritual instructions, Guru ji introduced the following social reforms: he forbade the custom of Sati, where the wife burnt herself alive when her husband died. He was against seclusion of women and Purdah i.e., women wearing veils. He encouraged the remarriage of women who lost their husbands, and he encouraged inter-caste marriages.

Visit of the Moghul Emperor Akbar, the Great
Akbar suceeded Humayun and tried to create unity among Hindus and Muslims. The buildings of his time reflect an integration of Indian and Islamic architecture. He also created the Urdu language that is a combination of Farsi and Hindi. ("Urdu" means an army.) He married a Rajput Hindu princess. Akbar came to visit Guru Amar Das. He had to share the meals in the Langar, (Community dining), sitting with all the Sangat. He wanted to grant land to Guru ji, but he refused, saying that Waheguru provides everything and he did not need anything. Akbar insisted that Guru ji's daughter Bhani ji was like a daughter to him. Therefore he gave the land grant in her name. Baba Budha ji managed the land and used the

proceedings for the Langar and other services.

Guru Amar Das wrote Anand Sahib (the song of bliss), which the Sikhs recite every day. Six stanzas from this Bani are sung at the end of every Sikh ceremony.

THE ANAND SAHIB

anand bhea mri mae

I am in ecstasy, O my mother, for I have found my True Guru.
I have found the True Guru with spiritual equanimity,
My mind vibrates with the music of bliss.
The jewelled melodies and their related celestial
Harmonies have come to sing the Word of the Shabad[1];
The Divine dwells within the minds of those,
Who sing the Shabad.
Says Nanak, I am in ecstasy for I have found my True Guru.

eh man meria tu sada rauh hari nale

O my mind, remain always with the Divine.
Remain always with the Divine,
O my mind, and all sufferings will be forgotten.
He will accept You as His own,
And all your affairs will be perfectly arranged.
The Divine is all powerful to do all things,
So why forget Him from your mind?
Says Nanak, O my mind, remain always with the Divine.

sache sahiba kia nahi ghar tere

O my True Master,
What is there which is not in Your celestial home?
Every thing is in Your home;

---

1. Shabad: Poetical compositions inspired by Divine Love.
Shabad literally means word.

They receive unto whom You give.
Constantly singing Your Praises and Glories,
Your Naam is enshrined in the mind.
The Divine melody of the Shabad vibrates for those,
Within whose minds the Naam abides.
Says Nanak, O my True Master,
What is there which is not in Your house?

sacha naam mera adharo

The True Naam is my only support.
The True Naam is my only support; it satisfies all hunger.
It has brought peace and tranquility to my mind.
It has fulfilled all my desires.
I am forever a sacrifice to the Guru,
Who possesses such glorious greatness.
Says Nanak, listen, O Saints; enshrine love for the Shabad.
The True Naam is my only support.

vaje panch sabad tit ghar subhage

The Panch Shabad, the five primal sounds,
Vibrate in that blessed house.
In that blessed house, the Shabad vibrates;
He infuses His almighty power into it.
Through You, we subdue the five demons of desire,
And slay Death, the torturer.
Those who have such pre-ordained
Destiny are attached to Naam.
Says Nanak, they are at peace,
And the unstruck music vibrates within themselves.
-Sri Guru Amar Das ji, SGGS - P. 917

anand suno vadhbhagio

Listen to the song of bliss,
O most fortunate ones.
All your longings shall be fulfilled.

123

I have obtained the Supreme Divine,
And all sorrows have been forgotten.
Pain, illness and suffering have departed,
Listening to the True Bani.
The Saints and their friends are in ecstasy,
Knowing the Perfect Guru.
Pure are the listeners, and pure are the speakers,
The True Guru is all pervading and permeating.
Prays Nanak, touching the Guru's Feet,
The unstruck sound of the celestial
Music vibrates and resounds. (25)

-Sri Guru Amar Das ji, SGGS - P. 922

Guru Amar Das ji wrote that knowing the true nature of oneself is to
know Waheguru.

man tu jot sarup hai

Mind, you are a Spark of Divine Light,
So grasp the True nature of your being.
The Creator is ever with you;
Through the Guru's teachings rejoice in His presence.
By grasping your own nature,
You have grasped the Supreme One
You shall lose the illusion of otherness.
You shall abide in peace, honored, and acceptable.
Nanak says: O my mind, you are an image of the Divine,
Grasp the True Source of your being. (25)

-Sri Guru Amar Das ji, SGGS - P. 441

Sri Guru Granth Sahib contains 885 of his poetical compositions. He was
73 when he became the Guru and served for 22 years. He was 95 years
old when he died. He had two sons-in-law. He transferred the Divine
Light to the younger son-in-law, Jetha ji, who excelled in devotion and
Sewa of the Guru and the Sangat.Ramdas bacame the fourth Guru.

4. SRI GURU RAMDAS JI

(1534 - 1581)

Guru Ramdas ji was born in Lahore on September 24, 1534. When Guru Amar Das ji passed the Light on to him, he told Guru Ramdas ji to establish another place for Sikh instructions. He should excavate a pool, where the visitors could bathe themselves before Naam meditation, recitation of Gurbani, and joining the Sangat for kirtan and Diwan.

Guru Ramdas ji established a new village called Guru Ka Chack, now known as Amritsar. He began excavation of the pool.

There was a Kardar, or a magistrate of Patti, who had five beautiful daughters. Four were married, and the youngest one was unmarried. One day, the five sisters were coming home after bathing and enjoying their father's country home. On the way, they came across a group of Sadhus who were singing Asa Di Var. They listened to the eighth Sloak that said,

> "God is the cherisher and Lord of all.
> He is the Cause of causes.
> He settles everything in motion,
> And holds everything in His power.
> It is the one Creator who destroys and preserves,
> Who produces and cherishes." (11)

The four sisters came home and became busy in their daily routine. The youngest one stayed back, and gave away whatever jewelry or money she had on her. She started the recitation of Naam and Gurbani. One day, their father asked them who provided them with all the luxuries of living. The four of them acknowledged that it was their father, but the youngest did not say anything. When the father asked what she thought, she replied, "Waheguru provides for all," including him. It enraged the father. He

125

thought she was a very thankless child.

He found a crippled man who suffered from leprosy, and married her to him. She took it as Waheguru's Bhana (Will) and started a very devoted and loving life with her husband. She went from door to door begging to feed them. One day, her husband said to her that he was a cripple leper. People shunned him, but she was so kind and loving to him. He must have done a lot of wrong in his previous lives to be given this diseased body, and he was not doing much good in this life, either. If he could go on a pilgrimage and wash away his past misdeeds, he might be saved from this suffering.

The devoted wife took him to extensive pilgrimages including Hardwar and Benaras, but to no avail. While they were returning home, they stopped in Guru Ka Chak. She left her husband under the cool shade of a Ber tree beside a pool of water and went away to beg for food.

While she was away, the husband saw a strange sight. Two crows were fighting with each other because one of them had a morsel of food in his beak. While they were fighting, the food fell into the pond. The crows dove in to get the food. Lo and behold, they were transformed into white swans and they flew away. The husband rolled himself into the pool. He became a completely able-bodied, handsome man, except one finger, which he kept out of water to hold onto a branch of the Ber tree.

When the wife returned, he reached out to her, but she was flabbergasted. She thought this person had murdered her husband and was making illicit advances toward her. Some onlookers told them to go to Guru Ramdas, who was sitting under a tree nearby, and he could settle the matter. When they went before Guru ji, he asked the man to dip his diseased finger in the pool, and it was completely healed. The couple rejoiced and stayed in Guru ji's service. He started working on the excavation of the pool. When her father heard about it, he began to serve the Guru Ghar and started a life of devotion to Naam.

The pool became known Amrit Sarowar (The Nector Pool). Guru Ka Chak began to flourish as a trade center, and got its present name Amritsar. The Ber tree is still there by the bank of the Sarowar surrounding the Golden Temple. It is called Dukh Bhanjni Beri (The Beri Tree that absolves all suffering).

To continue the development of Amritsar and spread the message of Guru Nanak, Guru Ramdas ji sent messengers to different parts of the country. They were called "Masands," a word derived from the word used by chiefs in Afghanistan. The chiefs were called Masand-e-Ali. For some time, these Masands served the Guru Ghar and provided spiritual instructions. After a while, they began to use money for their own comforts and led a self-indulgent life. Their services were discontinued by the Sixth Guru Hargobind ji.

Bhai Gurdas, whose Vaars (ballads) and Kabits are called the key to the understanding of Gurbani, was inspired by Guru Ramdas ji to the Sikh practice. Guru Ramdas ji described the daily spiritual routine of a Sikh as follows:

gur satgur ka jo sikh akhae

He who deems himself a Sikh of the True Guru
Rises before sunrise and contemplates the Naam.
In the early hours of the morning he rises and bathes
And cleanses his soul in a tank of nectar,
As he repeats Naam the Guru taught him.

Thus he washes away the misdeeds of his soul.
Then at dawn he sings the hymns of the Guru.
And throughout all the busyness of the day
He holds in his heart the Naam.
He who repeats Naam with every breath
Such a Sikh is indeed dear to the Guru.
The Sikh that wins the favor of the Beloved
Has received the gift of the Naam from the Guru.
Nanak seeks to kiss the dust under the feet of such a Sikh
Who meditates on Naam and inspires others to do so
Those who worship You become what you are.
                              -Sri Guru Ramdas ji, SGGS - P.305-6

Guru Ramdas ji wrote Lavan, which were later adopted for the Sikh wedding (the circumambulation of the bride and the bridegroom around Sri Guru Granth Sahib). During a Hindu wedding, the bride and the groom circumambulate around the sacred fire.

The word "Lavan" may be a derivative of the word "Launa" i.e. to employ someone or to attach someone to somebody. It could mean the attachment of two persons, bride and the groom. In Gurbani, lavan describes the attachment to Naam. The four stanzas of the four Lavan describe the spiritual development and the individual's union with the Divine. Each individual is merged with the Divine and they spiritually merge with each other as bride and bridegroom.

dhan pir seh na akhian

Wife and husband are not
The ones who sit together.
One Light in two forms,
They are the ones called wife and husband.
                              -Sri Amar Das ji, SGGS - P. 788

During a Sikh wedding, the Granthi (who reads Sri Guru Granth Sahib) reads one Lavan at a time. The Kirtanists start singing it after the reading. The husband and wife walk around Sri Guru Granth Sahib toward a spiritual union with Waheguru and with each other. The girl's brothers and/or cousins stand around Guru Granth Sahib, symbolizing that the couple can depend on family support on their spiritual journey, and the fulfillment of their social obligations. The couple circumambulates around Sri Guru Granth Sahib four times while the following four Lavan are sung one at a time:

THE MARRIAGE HYMNS (LAVAN)

har pehladi lanv parvirt

By the first nuptial vow,
The Divine shows you His Ordinance
For the daily duties of wedded life:
The Scriptures are the Word of the Divine,
Learn righteousness through them,
And the Divine will free you from misdeeds.
Hold fast to righteousness, contemplate Naam,
Fixing it in your memory as the scriptures have prescribed.
Devote yourselves to the Perfect and True Guru,
And all your misdeeds shall depart.
Fortunate are those whose minds
Are imbued with the Sweetness of Naam,
To them happiness comes without effort;
The devotee Nanak proclaims
That in the first circling
The marriage rite has begun.

By the second nuptial circling,
You are to understand that the Divine
Has caused you to meet the True Guru,
The fear in your hearts has departed.
The debris of selfishness in your minds is washed away,

By having the fear of Divine and by singing Its praises.
I stand before It with reverence,
The Creator is the soul of the universe:
There is nothing that It does not pervade.
Within and outside of us, there is One Creator only:
In the company of Saints
Are heard the songs of rejoicing.
The devotee Nanak proclaims
That in the second circling
Unstruck Divine Music is heard.

In the third circling,
There is a longing for the Divine
And detachment from the world.
In the company of the Saints,
By our great good fortune,
We encounter the Divine.
The Beloved is found in Its purity
Through the singing of Shabads.
By great good fortune we have
The company of the Saints
Wherein is told the story
Of the Ineffable Creator.
Naam echoes in the heart.
Echoes and absorbs us;
We repeat Naam,
Being blessed by a fortunate destiny
Written on our foreheads.
The devotee Nanak proclaims
That in the third circling
The love of Divine has been awakened in the heart.

In the fourth circling,
The mind reaches to knowledge of the Divine
And It is inwardly grasped:
Through the Grace of the Guru
We have attained with ease the Divine;

The sweetness of the Beloved
Pervades our body and soul.
Dear and pleasing is the Beloved to us:
Night and day our minds are fixed on It.
By exalting the Creator.
We have attained It.
The fruit our hearts desire;
The Beloved has finished Its work.
The soul, the spouse delights in the Beloved's Naam.
Felicitations fill our minds.
The Naam rings in our hearts:
The Divine is united with Its Devotee.
The heart of the Bride flowers with Naam.
The devotee Nanak proclaims
That in the fourth circling
We have found the Eternal Beloved. (25)

-Sri Guru Ramdas ji, SGGS - P.773-74

Guru ji's first cousin Sahari Mal came to invite Guru ji to grace the occasion of his son's wedding. Guru ji did not want to miss being with the Sangat. He was also busy with Amritsar development work. He told his cousin that there are always many Sikhs who accompany him wherever he goes. It will create an unnecessary burden for the bride's family to receive so many guests, therefore, it would be better if one of his sons went instead of him.

He asked his eldest son, Prithi Chand, who refused and made excuses. In fact, he did not want to go away, lest he be deprived of Guruship in his absence. Guru ji asked his second son, Mahadev, who spent most of his time in total detachment from worldly affairs. He declined, saying that he had no interest in worldly affairs. Then Guru ji asked his youngest son, Arjan Dev. He obeyed his father, even though he did not want to be away from him. He was told not to return until he was sent for. When he did not receive any message, he wrote the following letter:

mera man loche gur darsan tain

My soul longs for a sight of the Guru;
It cries like the Chatrik for raindrops.
My thirst is not quenched,
And I have no rest without a
Sight of the dear saint.
I am a sacrifice, to a sight of the Guru,
The dear saint. (11)

His brother Prithi Chand intercepted the letter. His father never received it. He wrote the following second letter:

tera mukh sohawa

Your face is beautiful,
The sound of your words gives spiritual equanimity.
It is long since I have seen my Guru.
Blessed is the land where you dwell,
O my saint, friend, and Guru.
I am a sacrifice to the holy Guru,
My Divine friend. (11)

His brother, Prithi Chand, intercepted this letter also and it never reached his father. He wrote the following third letter:

ik ghari na milte

When I was separated from you for a moment,
It seemed like dark ages.
When shall I now meet you, O my Beloved?
I cannot pass the night,
Sleep comes not without beholding the Guru's court.
I am a sacrifice to that court of the True Guru. (11)

The messenger was able to sneak to his father the third letter without being seen by Prithi Chand.

Guru Ramdas ji, seeing that the letter was numbered three, recovered the other two from Prithi Chand. Guru ji sent for his son Arjan Dev to return from Lahore. On arrival, Guru Ramdas ji asked him to complete his writing. He narrated the following fourth verse extemporaneously:

bhag hoa gur sant milaia

It is my good fortune to have met the saint Guru,
And I have found the Immortal Divine in my own home.
May I serve you and never again be separated
From you for an instant!
Nanak is your slave.
I am a sacrifice, And my soul is a sacrifice unto you: (11)
                    -Sri Guru Arjan Dev ji, SGGS - P. 96-97

It is clear from the above letters that Arjan Dev ji was already totally devoted to Waheguru, and saw no difference between Waheguru and his father who manifested Waheguru's Light. The letters are as much a longing for Waheguru as for his father. Guru Ramdas ji chose his youngest son Arjan Dev ji. He was only 18 years old when he took over the responsibilities of Guruship. Guru Ramdas ji went back to Goindwal Sahib and left his body to merge with the Divine Light.

koi an milavai mera pritam piara

I will be a slave of him, Who brings the Beloved for my tryst,
I longed to glimpse the Beloved.
By Divine Grace I met the Guru and
I attained Contemplation of Naam.

Beloved, when I am happy, I shall worship You only:
When I suffer, I shall not forget You.
Though you should cause me to hunger
I would live like a man fully fed.
Through my suffering I would feel joy. (25)
                    -Sri Guru Ramdas ji, SGGS - P. 757

5. SRI GURU ARJAN DEV JI

(1563 - 1606)

Guru Arjan Dev ji was born on April 15, 1563 in Goindwal Sahib. Guru
Arjan Dev ji accompanied his father to Goindwal Sahib to be with him
when he breathed his last. When Guru Arjan Dev ji returned to Amritsar,
his eldest brother Prithi Chand declared that being the eldest, he was the
rightful heir to Guruship. In his Haumain he forgot that Gurus passed on
the Light on the basis of merit and not as worldly property. Nevertheless,
Prithi Chand and some of his associates intercepted the Sikhs who brought
food and offerings for the Guru Ghar(house) to continue the free Langar
(Community dining) and spiritual instructions from the Guru.

Guru Arjan Dev ji and his wife Mata Ganga ji continued the Langar even
though, at times, all they had to eat were parched grains. When Bhai Gurdas
ji returned from Agra to visit his maternal nephew Guru Arjan Dev, he
was quite pained to see the state of affairs. He approached Baba Budha ji
at Pipli Sahib. Baba Budha ji and other Sikhs intervened to resolve the
situation.

Guru Arjan Dev ji continued the development of Amritsar that his father
Guru Ramdas ji started. He built a Gurdwara in the middle of the pool
and called it Harmandir (Divine Temple). He invited his friend, Muslim
Faqir Saint Mian Meer to lay the foundation stone. The Gurdwara has
four doors welcoming people from four directions and from all four
castes. In the 19th century Maharaja Ranjit Singh made the temple ornate
and decorated the outside with gold plated material. In the West, it is
known by its appearance as the Golden Temple. The Sikhs call it either Sri
Darbar Sahib or Sri Harmandir Sahib. There is a Guru Ramdas *Sarai*
(Inn) for the pilgrims to stay free of charge and eat at the free Langar.

There are no lectures at Harmandir Sahib. From 4 a.m. to midnight, there is a continuous Gurbani Kirtan. The pilgrims stay to listen to Gurbani as long as they wish. The sixth Guru Hargobind built the Akal Takht (The Seat of the Eternal) opposite the causeway entrance to Harmandir Sahib, which is the first seat of Sikh religious organization. This is where Sri Guru Hargobind Sahib conducted temporal affairs.

Guru Arjan Dev ji collected all the writings of the first four Gurus and 29 saints from all religions, different castes, different parts of India and socio- economic classes. Guru ji edited the writings and Bhai Gurdas ji transcribed them. He had the Parkash (Manifestation by opening the holy book) of Adi Granth, now known as Sri Guru Granth Sahib, in Sri Harmandir Sahib. He also instructed the Sikhs to do the Kirtan. Guru ji always gave a higher status and respect to Sri Guru Granth Sahib because it is considered:

Pothi Parmeshar Ka Roop

The Holy Book is the manifestation of the Divine

Sri Guru Granth Sahib contains the poetry of loving devotion to Naam and Waheguru, no matter what name you use for the Divine Creator. It beckons people to avoid hypocritical rituals and practices. Without loving devotion to Naam and selfless service of Its creation, everything is futile.

EMPEROR JAHANGIR

By the time emperor Jahangir succeeded to the Moghul throne after Akbar the Great, the Moghul empire was firmly established throughout India. He was famous for his just rule (Adal-E-Jahangiri).

135

At the same time, the Sikh Gurus were known all over India. People of all faiths, from all parts of India came to have audience with the Guru. Amritsar was a thriving trading center and a place for pilgrimage. It raised concerns in Jahangir's mind. He wrote the following in his autobiography Tuzuk-I-Jehangiri:

"A Hindu, Arjan by name, lived in the garb of a pir and Sheikh and had captivated the hearts of many simple minded Hindus and stupid Muslims by his ways and means —- For three or more generations they had kept this shop going. For years I have been thinking of either putting an end to the false traffic or that he (Guru) should be brought into the fold of Islam".(11)

While the emperor had his concerns, the local Brahmins and others felt a threat to their vested interest, because the Gurus were against the caste system and idol worship. Jahangir's son, Khusro, rebelled against him and escaped to Punjab. On his way, he came to visit Guru Arjan Dev ji. Anybody who gave shelter and comfort to Khusro was considered an enemy of the state. This gave an excuse to the local administrators and the ruling class. Jahangir ordered his arrest and execution. Chandu carried a grudge against the Guru Ghar. He requested that he be given the responsibility to carry out the execution, and he planned a most torturous murder of Guru ji. He made him sit on a hot griddle, and poured hot sand on his body.

Faqir Mian Mir, who was the spiritual guide to Emperor Jahangir's family, could not bear such torture. He was also a great friend of Guru ji. He had laid the foundation stone of Sri Harmandir Sahib. He beseeched Guru ji that he should be allowed to approach Jahangir and tell him the truth that he has been misinformed and should stop these atrocities. Guru ji said it is Divine Will and asked Faqir Mian Mir to close his eyes and see with his inner spiritual eye.

What Faqir Mian Mir saw was **that the person who was pouring the hot sand and the person who was sitting on the hot griddle were the same.**

Guru ji asked that he be taken to bathe in the river Ravi. As his blistered body immersed in the cool river water, he left his body and merged with the Divine. He passed on the Light to his only son Hargobind. Guru Arjan Dev ji wrote the most Bani. There are 2304 of his compositions in Sri Guru Granth Sahib written in variety of poetical forms and languages.

6. SRI GURU HARGOBIND JI

(1595 - 1644)

Sri Guru Hargobind ji was born in Amritsar on June 14, 1595. At the time of his father Sri Guru Arjan Dev ji's Martyrdom, he was only 11 years old. At this tender age, he had to take over the religious instructions of the Sikhs. He had to carry out the responsibilities of the Guru in a hostile environment created by the jealous Chandu and the fearful rulers of Punjab who connived together to torture Guru Arjan Dev ji to death.

At the time, Baba Budha ji was going to perform the ceremony to establish him the Guru by conferring upon him Seli (a woolen woven thread one wears around the neck or around the turban or a cap), and a head dress. Guru Hargobind Sahib requested that he should change the ceremony. He wanted to replace Seli with a Gatra (the cloth belt for wearing a sword). He wanted to wear two swords; one for Miri (temporal power), and the other for Piri (spiritual living). He realized that one has to protect the oppressed against unjust rulers.

Baba Nanak instructed Sikhs to be householders who earn an honest living and meditate on Naam (Waheguru Simran). As householders, they should also have the strength to defend themselves against injustice and oppression. Therefore, Guru Hargobind Sahib wanted his Sikhs to be strong warriors.

As soon as he became the Guru, he sent messages to his Sikhs that they should bring horses and weapons as offerings. He began training his Sikhs in martial arts and raised a small army. There were a few battles between the Sikhs and the armies of Moghul Governors of Lahore and Jallandhar, and the Moghuls were repelled.

The Sikh's call a sword a "Kirpan," which means, by the Grace (of Waheguru) or blessing. By the Grace of Waheguru, it is blessed for the protection of the oppressed and helpless victims. If it is used offensively or for material or for sectarian gains, then it is no longer a Sikh Kirpan, it is just a sword. The Guru's power is no more with us. Sikhs live by Bhai Gurdas ji's definition of non-violence:

> *Mat hondi hoi iana*
> *Taan honed hoi nitana*
> *Unhonda aap vanda-e*
> *Koi aisa bhagat sada-e*

Being intelligent maintains childlike innocence
Having strength remains non-violent
He shares more then he has
That is the person worthy of being called a saint.

Guru Hargobind Sahib also initiated the Sikh ceremony of dealing with a death in the family. When his father Sri Guru Arjan Dev ji died, he asked Bhai Budha ji to start reading Sri Adi Granth Sahib, and this reading was completed in ten days. At the time of completion of reading Sri Adi Granth Sahib there was a Bhog Ceremony with Asa Di Var Kirtan and partaking of Langar by the Sangat. This ceremony continues in Sikh families to this day, and the mourning period ends after the *Bhog*.

There was a Qazi who beat up his daughter every day. Faqir Mian Mir (the friend of Guru Arjan Dev ji) was a friend of the Qazi family. His daughter, Kaulan, used to hear Guru Arjan Dev ji's Shabads from Faqir Mian Mir. She could not tolerate the beatings of her father. She left her family in Lahore and took refuge with Guru Hargobind Sahib. The Qazi did his best to get her back; he even approached Emperor Jahangir, but to no avail. Whoever takes refuge under Guru's protection, no power on earth can harm. Kaulan devoted her life to serve the Guru Ghar. One day she brought all her jewelry and possessions and wanted Guru Sahib to use them for religious purposes. Considering her devotion and service, Guru Sahib got a Sarovar (water tank) excavated in her name where pilgrims could bathe. It is called Kaulsar. Sri Guru Hargobind ji got excavated four water tanks. Now there are five water tanks in Amritsar City: Amritsar, Bibeksar, Ramsar, Santokhsar, and Kaulsar.

Emperor Jahangir and Sri Guru Hargobind Sahib

Chandu and his associate rulers of Lahore began to incite Jahangir against Sri Guru Hargobind ji. They told him that Guru Sahib was much more dangerous than his father, Guru Arjan Dev ji. He had raised an army to avenge his father's death and was converting Muslims to become his Sikhs. In fact, one of his favorite soldiers was a Muslim Painde Khan. Jahangir's Minister Wazir Khan was in fact a Sikh at heart. Guru Arjan Dev ji saved his life from a fatal disease. He tried to tell the truth that Guru Sahib was neither vindictive, nor did he have any temporal ambitions.

Guru ji was 17 years old when Jahangir sent Wazir Khan to bring Guru Sahib to Delhi. Baba Budha ji, his mother Mata Ganga ji, and other senior Sikhs were quite concerned about this invitation. He was the only son, and they thought they would never see him again. Nevertheless, Guru Sahib decided to accept the invitation to visit Emperor Jahangir in Delhi.

Emperor Jahangir received him with respect. He saw him as a young man only 17 years old, and asked him many questions about spiritual and religious matters. One question and Guru Sahib's answer is given below as an example, narrated by Macauliffe (11, Vol. IV)

> "What is the essential difference between
> Hindus who worship Ram Narayan,

Parbrahm, and Parmeshar and the
Musalmans who pray to Allah, the
Bounteous Lord?

The Guru replied with the following Shabad of Guru Arjan Dev ji in
Raag Ramkali:

The Bounteous One is the Cause of causes;
The Merciful One cherishes all.
Allah is invisible and unequalled.
He alone is God great and infinite.
I bow to one God, the Creator:
The Creator pervades every place.
As Makho He is Lord and Life of the world,
The Destroyer of fear; worship Him in your heart.
Whether known as Rikhikesh, Gopal, Gobind, Or Mukand,
You alone, O God, are the kind Master.
You are at once Pir, Prophet, and Shaikh.
Master of hearts You dispenses justice.
You are holier than Quaran and the other Muhammadan books.
Whether as Narayan, Narhar, or the Compassionate,
You pervade every heart and are the heart's support.
As Vasdev you dwell in every place.
Your sport is not understood.
You are the Bestower of kindness and mercy.
Grant us devotion and worship of you, O Creator.
Said Nanak, when the Guru
has removed (the veil of) superstition,
Allah and Parbrahm are the same.

The Emperor and Guru Sahib spent a lot of time together. Queen Noor
Jahan came to visit him with her Ranis and maids. Everyone enjoyed the
spiritual presence of this handsome youth. Whenever the Emperor traveled, Guru Sahib's tent was pitched next to him.

Once they went on a hunting expedition together. While the "drum beaters" were chasing the animals toward the hunting party, suddenly a tiger leaped toward Emperor Jahangir. Guru Hargobind ji jumped off his horse and received the tiger's paw on his shield, and stabbed his chest with his sword. **Thus, he saved the life of the Emperor, for which the Emperor was grateful. Gurus were totally Nirvair (devoid of enmity). He was the same Jahangir Emperor who had ordered the execution of his father Guru Arjan Dev ji.**

After some time Emperor Jahangir came down with a serious illness. He invited some Brahmin Vaids (physicians) and astrologers to find a remedy. It is said that, old, resentful and fearful of Guru Ghar, Chandu, bribed the Brahmin astrologer. He told the Emperor that he was ill because of Guru Sahib's presence, and he should be imprisoned; that would make him well.

Jahangir ordered Guru Sahib to proceed to Gwaliar fort, where he would be imprisoned. Guru Sahib left for Gwaliar with a contingent of his Sikh soldiers. He kept five Sikhs with him and told the rest of them to go back to Punjab. Guru ji and five of his Sikhs were imprisoned with 52 other political prisoner Rajas. In prison, he continued his Simran routine and the Rajas loved him for his spiritual presence and instruction.

Emperor Jahangir's minister, Wazir Khan, found out about Chandu's conspiracy to send Guru Sahib to prison in Gwaliar fort. He told the Emperor the truth, and the Emperor was quite regretful, and ordered Guru Sahib's release. When Wazir Khan brought the news of Guru Sahib's release to Gwaliar fort, the Rajas were very sad. Guru Sahib's presence had brought great joy to the Rajas. Observing this, Guru Sahib told Wazir Khan that he would not leave the fort until all 52 Rajas were also freed. When the Emperor was given this message, he said that those Rajas who could hold on to his shirttails could follow him outside the fort. Guru Sahib got himself a robe tailored with 52 corners. When he came out, all 52 Rajas held onto his robe and they were set free. Since then, he was known as **Bandi Chhor, The Liberator.**

On Guru Sahib's return, Jahangir told him he was going to Kashmir to recover from his illness. The beauty of Kashmir mountains, fresh air, and peace and quiet would be life nurturing. He invited Guru Sahib to accompany him, and Guru Sahib agreed. On the way, they visited Goindval, where Guru Amar Das ji used to live. When they reached Amristar, Guru Sahib wanted to part company and go home. Emperor Jahangir wanted to visit Harmandir Sahib (Golden temple). The Empress Noor Jahan as well as other Ranis accompanied him, and also visited Mata Ganga ji. Emperor Jahangir wanted to take responsibility to complete Harmandir Sahib and Akal Takht, but Guru Sahib declined his offer, saying that it was Waheguru's abode; no one can own it. If you pay for it, then it establishes your ownership; all the people own it. Even now, when you are doing Par karma (Circumambulation) in Harmandir Sahib, you will notice the names of different persons on marble pavement. It is truly a people's place and Waheguru's abode.

Live In Guru's Bhana (Divine Will):

Guru Sahib's son Baba Atal was nine years old. He once noticed that to light fire in the hearth, one used small splinters, then placed the bigger logs on after the splinters ignited. Seeing this, he realized that he was little, therefore, he should waste no more time. Who knows when Waheguru may call upon him to leave his body. He was immersed in Naam Simran ever since.

Baba Atal had a playmate, Mohan. They played tag and other games. The next day it was Mohan's turn to tag the kids. Unfortunately, he was bitten by a cobra and died. When Baba Atal went to his house, he saw everyone lamenting his friends death. He walked up to where he was lying and said, " You can't leave us without keeping your turn in the game," and revived Mohan.

When Guru Sahib found out about this event, he told Baba Atal that one should never use supernatural powers to interfere with Waheguru's Bhana. Baba Atal went to a secluded place, drew a sheet over him, and left his body and went to Sach Khaud (The region of Truth). Now, there is a nine story monument near Sri Darbar Sahib (golden temple) called Baba Atal.

Sant Sipahi (Saint Soldier)

Guru Hargobind Sahib was returning from a hunting expedition with his warrior Sikhs. A Faqir saw him, and questioned his life style. He thought Guru ji was a disgrace to Baba Nanak's Guru Ghur. He said Baba Nanak was a Tyagi (one who has renounced the world) and a saint, while Guru Sahib was dressed like royalty and accompanied by warriors.

Guru Sahib replied to him humbly that Baba Nanak had not preached renunciation. He considered the householder's life as the greatest yoga. The outworldly warrior robes are to protect the freedom of religious practice and the oppressed people. **The true renunciation is to renounce one's Haumain and meditate on Naam.**

Sri Guru Hargobind ji had five sons: Baba Gurdita, Suraj Mal, Ani Rai, Baba Atal and Teg Bahadur.

Sri Guru Hargobind Sahib departed for Sach Khand on March 19, 1644 and passed on Baba Nanak's Light to Sri Guru Har Rai ji, the second son of Baba Gurdita.

7. SRI GURU HAR RAI JI

(1630 – 1661)

Sri Guru Har Rai ji was the grandson of Sri Guru Hargobind Sahib. He was born on February 26, 1630 to his mother Mata Nihal Kaur and father Gurditta ji. Baba Gurditta was the eldest son of Sri Guru Hargobind Sahib. He had two sons, Dhir Mal and Har Rai. Gurditta ji died young. Sri Guru Hargobind Sahib chose Gurditta's younger son Har Rai, because Dhirmal was full of Haumain and did not lead a Gurmukh life. Therefore, Sri Guru Har Rai Sahib received Baba Nanak's Light and became the Seventh Guru of the Sikhs at the young age of thirteen.

Guru ji continued the Sant Sipahi tradition of his grandfather Sri Guru Hargobind Sahib. He was a handsome warrior with a very kind heart. He started a free hospital and a dispensary in Kirat pur Sahib. He also initiated the currently prevailing tradition that Guru Ka Langar (The Guru's blessed free food) should be served to everyone, whenever a person arrives for it. It should be open 24 hours, and not time bound.

Emperor Shah Jahan and Guru Har Rai Sahib

Emperor Shah Jahan, who is famous for building the Taj Mahal, had four sons. Dara Shjkoh was the heir apparent and was the favorite of the emperor. He kept him next to him. His second son, Shujah Muhammad, was the Governor of Bengal. His third son Aurangzeb, was the governor of Dakhan. His fourth son, Murad Bakash was the Governor of Gujrat. Auangzeb was very cunning. He wanted Dara Shikoh to be out of his way. He connived to mix tiger's whiskers in Dara Shikoh's food. The prince became terribly ill. No Vaids, Pirs or Faqirs could heal him. The remedy they suggested was only available in Guru Sahib's dispensary, which was known to his minister. Shah Jahan wrote the following letter to Sri

Guru Har Rai Sahib,

"Thy predecessor, the holy Baba Nanak granted sovereignty to the Emperor Babar, the founder of my dynasty. Guru Angad was exceedingly well disposed to his son, the Emperor Humayun, and Guru Amar Das removed many difficulties from my grandfather Akbar's path. I regret the same friendly relations did not subsist between Guru Hargobind and myself, and that misunderstandings were caused by interference of strangers. For this I was not to blame. My son Dara Shikoh is now very ill. His remedy is in thy hands. If thou giveth the myrobalan and the clove which are in thy storehouse, and add to them thy prayers, thou will confer abiding favor on me".

(11, Vol. IV)

When the Emperor's nobleman presented his letter to Guru ji, he addressed the Sangat quoting the following line from Asa Di Var:

"Why should they who come with hope depart disappointed".

"Behold, said the Guru, "with one hand man breaketh flowers, and with other hand he offereth them, but the flowers perfumes both hands alike. Although the axe cuts the Sandal tree, yet the Sandal perfumeth the axe. The Guru was in position of a tree which, though cut with a sharp axe, feels no anger and imputes no blame to the wood cutter, but ministers unto his wants."

(11, Vol. IV)

Guru Sahib sent the Emperor the requested remedies and added one of his own. Dara Shikoh recovered from his illness.

Emperor Aurangzeb And Guru Ji

Emperor Shah Jahan was taken ill. In the power struggle for the throne of Delhi, Aurangzeb was victorious. He defeated Dara Shikoh by making an alliance with Murad Baksh. Later on, Auragzeb imprisoned Murad Baksh and his ill father Shah Jahan. Shujah Muhammad fled after his defeat. Dara Shikoh escaped to Punjab. Aurangzeb sent a proclamation: If anybody would provide refuge to his rebellious brother, he would be severely punished. Dara Shikoh was a great admirer of Faqir Mian Mir, who was a close friend of Guru Ghar. The fifth Guru Sri Guru Arjan Dev ji had invited him to lay the foundation stone of Sri Harmandir Sahib (Golden Temple). Through Faqir Mian Mir, Dara Shikoh arranged a meeting with Guru Sahib. He had several reasons to meet Guru ji. First, he wanted to meet the Guru who saved his life. Second, he had studied both Islamic religious texts and Hindu scriptures. He was inclined like his ancestor Akbar the Great, and wanted to have religious discourse with the Guru. Third, he wanted his protection.

After he met the Guru Sahib, he renounced his ambition to regain the Delhi throne. He wanted to spend his life in spiritual pursuits. Aurangzeb's troops were in hot pursuit. Guru Sahib detained the Mughal troops until he had escaped to Multan and Bhakhar. He was betrayed by one of his men, captured and brought to Delhi, where he was executed. A signed petition from 300 Mullahs accused him of treason and not living up to Islamic traditions.

With the guidance of these self-serving fanatic Mullahs, Aurangzeb started to wipe out the Hindu religion. He destroyed the sacred idols in Mathura, Benaras and the temple of Brahma in Pushkar. Meantime, his fanatic advisors complained that Guru Sahib aided Dara Shikoh against the Emperor, and preached a religion different from Islam. Aurangzeb was incensed and wanted to send an army to arrest him. His advisors prevailed upon him to invite Guru Sahib to Delhi to persuade him to convert to Islam. If the Guru embraced Islam, then the rest would follow. If he did not accept Islam, then the Emperor could deal with him as he pleased. Therefore, Aurangzeb sent him the following letter:

Guru Nanak's house was the house of holy men. He treated friend and foe in the same way, but thou has not supported Dara Shikoh in his effort to obtain sovereignty. I have captured and put him to death, so he hath in no way benefited by thy assistance. But let bygones be bygones, and let us now be friends. Come to me. I am now enthroned as Emperor. I have a great desire to behold thee. Wherefore thou shouldst come to me without delay.

The Guru replied, "I have no business with thee that thou shouldst have summoned me. I am not a king who payeth thee tribute, nor do we stand in the relation of priest and disciple to each other, so wherefore hast thou summoned me? So far from my having conferred empire on Dara Shikoh, it was the eternal throne and umbrella of religion I conferred on him. He had no wish for territorial empire. The empire he hath obtained is imperishable. It is only he whom God loveth who can be like Dara Shikoh. If thou hast any doubt as to the empire Dara Shikoh hath obtained, meditate on him as thou goest to sleep, and thou shall have a vision of the reality."

(11, Vol. IV)

Aurangzeb dreamt that his brother was on a celestial throne and Aurangzeb was carrying garbage. He sent another reconciliatory invitation. The Sangat discussed the pros and cons of going to Delhi, but Guru ji said, "What you counsel is politic, but I have registered a vow that I will never look at the wicked Aurangzeb."

He knew the atrocities he had committed, and his ruthless, treacherous ways. Meanwhile his son Ram Rai, appeared and volunteered to go to Delhi. Guru ji instructed him not to indulge in miracles or to alter Gurbani. Ram Rai did indulge in miracles and altered Gurbani to please the Emperor. Guru ji banished him and never wanted to see his face again. Aurangzeb gave him a land grant in Doon Valley where he established his own Dehra (Sant Ashram). The city is now called Dehradoon.

Guru ji passed Baba Nanak's light to his younger son Harkrishan, who was only five years old at the time.

8. SRI GURU HARKRISHAN

(1656 -1664)

Born on July 7,1656 Sri Guru Harkrishan Sahib was the younger son of Sri Guru Har Rai Sahib. His brother, Ram Rai, complained to Emperor Auranzgeb that he was wrongfully deprived of Guruship. Aurangzeb asked Guru Harkrishan to visit him and explain why Guruship should not be conferred on his older brother.

Guru ji decided to go to Delhi but did not want to see Aurangzeb. On his way to Delhi, he imparted religious instructions to Sikhs who would go to visit him. When he arrived at Panjokhara, a Brahmin became very indignant. How could a seven year-old child be a Guru? Moreover, he took offense that his name was Harkrishan. Lord Krishna delivered the great spiritual message in Bhagwat Gita: if he is the Guru, he should interpret Bhagvat Gita. Guru ji put his loving hand on the head of an illiterate member of the Sikh Sangat and asked the Brahmin if he would ask any questions he had on his mind. The Brahmin was amazed at the eloquent interpretation of Gita coming from a known illiterate person. The Brahmin asked forgiveness for doubting the Guru. Guru ji blessed him and continued his journey to Delhi.

After reaching Delhi, he camped outside the city, where Gurdwara Bangla Sahib is constructed. Aurangzeb sent Raja Jai Singh to invite Guru Sahib to his Darbar. Guru Sahib told him that his father had instructed him that his older brother manage political affairs in the Emperors court. He was instructed to preach devotion to Sat Naam (True Name). He had no business in the Emperor's court. Aurangzeb sent his son to inquire how he explained his right to Guruship. Guru ji replied to the prince that Guruship is not a material property that can be inherited according to property rights. From the time of Baba Nanak, the Light is passed on to the person who the Guru considers the most spiritual soul. Guru Nanak chose his Sikh over his own sons, and that tradition continues. The prince was fully satisfied. Meantime, small pox broke out in Delhi, and throngs of people came to Guru ji to be healed. Guru ji contracted small pox and departed for Sachkhand on March 30, 1664 without ever seeing Emperor Aurangzeb. At the time of Guru ji's death, he said the Guru was in Baba Bakale.

9. SRI GURU TEGH BAHADUR JI
(1621 -1675)

Sri Guru Tegh Bahadur ji was the youngest son of Sri Guru Hargobind ji. He was born on April 16, 1621. He spent most of his life in meditation and wrote beautifully. One of his verses is given below:

Jo nar dukh mein dukh nahi maane

That man who in the midst of grief is free from grieving,
And free from fear, and free from the snare of delight,
Nor is covetous of gold that he knows to be dust,
Who is neither a backbiter nor a flatterer,
Nor has greed in his heart, nor vanity,
Nor any worldly attachment,
Who remains at his center unmoved by good and ill fortune.
Who is indifferent to the world's praise and blame
And discards every wishful fantasy
Accepting his lot in a disinterested fashion,
Not worked upon by lust or by wrath,
In such a man Divine dwells.
The man on whom the Grace of the Guru alights
Understands the way of conduct:
His soul, O Nanak, is merged with the Divine
As water mingles with water! (25)
                    -Sri Guru Teg Bahadur ji, SGGS - P.633

At the time of Sri Guru Harkrishan's death, he said, "Guru Baba Bakale." Guru is in the town of Baba Bakala, but he did not name his grand uncle. Since the time of Sri Guru Ramdas ji, the Gurus were from a Sodhi family. After hearing that Guru was in Baba Bakale, 22 Sodhis installed themselves as the Guru. Sri Guru Tegh Bahadur ji stayed in his meditation.

Guru Ladho Re (Found the Guru):

A merchant named Makhan Shah Labana used to carry goods in his sailboat. Once, when he was on his voyage from Gujarat, his boat was caught in a whirlpool during a great storm. He felt very helpless. In desperation, he prayed to Baba Nanak's Guru Ghar and promised that he would offer 500 Mohars (gold coins) as a token of his gratitude. His boat reached the destination without harm. He came to Punjab to fulfill his promise of the offering to the Guru. When he arrived in Baba Bakala, he found 22 Gurus. He was totally perplexed, and did not know whom to give the offering. He was a smart merchant. He thought to himself, if the Guru could heed his prayer from several hundred miles away, he would surely know what he had promised to the Guru as his offering. Therefore, he started offering two Mohars to each of the pretend Gurus. Everyone accepted the offering and blessed him. Makhan Shah was very dejected for not finding the one True Guru (Satguru).

He began to inquire if there were any other holy men living in that town. Someone said that there was Tegh Bahadur, who keeps to him self, does his farming chores and people hardly see him around. Makhan Shah went to his house and found Guru ji in meditation. After Guru ji opened his eyes and greeted his guest Makhan Shah, the merchant bowed before him and made an offering of two Mohars in front of Guru ji. Sri Guru Tegh Bahadur said that one should never make false promises. It does not behoove a person to make promises in adversity, and then not fulfill the promise after the adversity is over. You had vowed to make an offering of 500 Mohars, not two.

Makhan Shah was overjoyed. He went on the top of the house and started claiming in a loud voice, "Guru Ladho Re." The Sikhs were ultimately relieved to find who the True Guru was. Sri Guru Tegh Bahadur ji started the regular Gursangat Darbar and began giving spiritual instructions to the Sikhs.

Sacrifice For The Freedom Of Worship:

Meantime, Aurangzeb continued his campaign of terror and devastation of Hindu shrines and murdering Brahmins who would not accept Islam. One of the holiest shrines and a great center of learning is the Amarnath Temple in Kashmir. The great Pundits there took a delegation of Brahmins headed by Kirpa Ram[1] to Baba Nanak's Guru Ghar. Sri Guru Tegh Bahadur's son Gobind Rai was only nine years old. He asked his father why there was such a pandemonium in Gur Sangat Darbar. Guru Sahib told him that Emperor Aurangzeb was killing Lakhs (a hundred thousand) of people only because they have a different way of worship. Gobind Rai asked if there was a way out. Guru Sahib told his young son, if a truly spiritual person would be willing to sacrifice himself then these atrocities could be stopped. Gobind Rai exclaimed, who is more spiritual than you? Baba Nanak's light is manifested in you.

Sri Guru Tegh Bahadur was happy to see the spiritual strength of his little son who would offer his own father as a sacrifice to stop the atrocities committed in the name of Allah. Guru ji sent a message to Aurangzeb that Allah was not pleased by hurting people and destroying his creation.

He wanted to appear before Emperor Aurangzeb. If Emperor could convert him, all of India would be converted to Islam. Aurangzeb accepted his offer and sent for him. When Sri Guru Tegh Bahadur ji met Emperor Aruangzeb, there was no dialogue.

---

[1]Later on Kirpa Ram became Amrit Dhari Khalsa Kirpa Singh and stayed with Sri Guru Gobind Singh ji until he was killed in the battle of Chamkaur Sahib, along with three Payares (Beloved ones) and two sons of Sri Guru Gobind Singh.

The Emperor gave Guru Sahib the choice between death and Islam. He imprisoned Guru ji in a cage and displayed him in Chandni Chawk (Chandni Plaza) in Delhi in front of the Red Fort. He asked Guru ji to perform miracles as he had asked Ram Rai, who obliged the Emperor and was given the land grant in Dehradun. Guru ji refused and stayed in his meditation. Three of the Sikhs were murdered brutally in front of him. Bhai Daya Ram was boiled to death, Bhai Mati Das was sawed to death, Bhai Sati Das was burnt alive. On the third day, Guru ji was beheaded on November 11, 1675. Now there is a Gurdwara Sis Ganj where Guru ji was executed. Emperor Aurangzeb asked if anyone believed the way Guru ji did, he should come forward and claim his body. Nobody dared. At night, Bhai Jaita ji and Bhai Nagaia ji stole his body. Bhai Nagaia ji burnt his house to cremate the body. Gurdwara Rakab Gunj in New Delhi is built to commemorate this event. Bhai Jaita ji took his head to Anand Pur Sahib. Mata Gujri ji bowed and did the Parkarma (Circumambulation) around his head. She thanked Waheguru that Guru Sahib and the Sikhs lived up to their convictions (Sikhi Nibhai) and Waheguru protected their honor.

When his nine years old son Gobind Rai heard the story that no Sikh came forward to claim Guru ji's body, he said that it is not sufficient to have the right belief system and meditate on Naam; one should have the courage of one's convictions. Later on he gave his Sikhs the form of Khalsa. They stand out in millions because of their appearance. They could not, and they would not deny their love of Sat Naam and Waheguru.

It was a logical culmination of Guru Nanak's teachings that a Sikh is a householder. Living in this world a Sikh meets all his/her social and family obligations while all the time meditating on Naam. The protection of one's family and the oppressed is an obligation that a spiritual householder can not shirk. From the sixth Guru onward the Gurus introduced a Sikh as a spiritual warrior. Guru Gobind Singh gave the final form which is elaborated in the next chapter.

10. SRI GURU GOBIND SINGH JI: THE KHALSA
(1666-1708)

Sri Guru Nanak Dev ji integrated spirituality into the daily life of individuals. Prior to him, the people pursuing spirituality renounced the world, practiced austerities or became monks. Some Hindu clergy (Brahmin) and Muslim clergy (Mullahs) exploited and oppressed innocent people by engaging in hypocritical, ritualistic practices. The Hindus were divided into castes and the Brahmins became the custodians of their spiritual salvation.

In his nine manifestations prior to Sri Guru Gobind Singh ji, Guru Nanak Dev ji renewed spiritual awakening. The essence of all beings is the Creator. All of us come from the same Source and we merge back into it. Our Atma (soul) is a fragment of the Param Atma (the supreme soul, the Creator). The purpose of human life is to realize Waheguru within ourselves. With such Waheguru consciousness we discharge all social responsibilities. With loving devotion we serve the Divine and Creation. Divine is immanent as well as transcendental, and is well illustrated by Guru Gobind Singh ji in the following verse:

> Waheguru and the devotee are the same,
> There is no difference between them.
> As the wave springs up from water
> And merges back into it.
> -Sri Guru Gobind Singh ji, Bachitar Natak

What keeps us from seeing the spiritual unity of this universe is our Haumain ("I Am" consciousness i.e., I am the doer). The idea of being a Sikh is to alleviate the Haumain consciousness and replace it with cosmic Waheguru consciousness, to be in a state of eternal bliss while we are alive. As the fifth Guru Sri Guru Arjan Dev ji expressed:

156

The beloved is manifested in everyone.
Perceiving this, Nanak is in a state of bliss.

From such Waheguru consciousness, it logically flows that a Sikh does not discriminate against anyone for any reason. The Gurus not only expressed this unity in Gurbani, they created institutions of *Sangat* and *Pangat* (Everyone who goes to Gurdwara is required to partake of the blessed food sitting together - *Langar*). There could be no untouchables. No human being should oppress any other human being because of religion, class, status, gender, material position or quality of his/her deeds (Karma) in this world.

Grihasth Yoga (the Yoga of being a householder) is considered the highest spiritual achievement, living in Waheguru consciousness and discharging all our worldly responsibilities in an ever-present, loving devotion to Waheguru. In spite of our Haumain based Karma in this world, which creates pressure on us and provokes our Haumain to react in the same way and become distracted from Waheguru love, a Sikh maintains his/her state of spiritual equanimity (Sehaj). The Gurus were married, had children and participated in all extended family functions. Their brothers, at times, subjected some of them to jealousies. People who lived in Haumain consciousness tortured them. The fifth and ninth Gurus were brutally executed. The Sikh Gurus demonstrated throughout their lives, what Guru Nanak declared; that nothing in this world could deter him from his Love for Waheguru.

dehi dukh laya paap garab do-e raah

Though my body be crippled with disease,
Though the relentless stars bring endless misfortune on me,
Though bloody tyrants fill my soul with terror,
Though all these miseries be at once heaped on my head,

157

Even then, my Beloved, I shall praise you:
And I shall not grow weary of exalting Your Naam. (25)

Sri Guru Nanak Dev ji, SGGS - P.142

Guru Nanak Dev ji described the state of the ruling class:

Kal kaati raje kasai

This age is like a drawn Sword,
The kings are butchers.
Goodness had taken wings and flown
In the dark night of falsehood.
I espy not the moon of Truth anywhere
I grope after truth and am bewildered.

I see no path in the darkness.
It is the obstinacy with which man
Clings to his petty Haumain
That causes this anguish.
Nanak asks: Where is the path of salvation? (25)

-Sri Guru Nanak Dev ji, SGGS - P.145

For nearly two centuries, the nine Gurus created spiritual integrity as house-holders in the habitants of India. The sixth Guru Hargobind ji brought to Sikhs an awareness that temporal power should also be guided by spiritual consciousness. Otherwise, "power corrupts and absolute power corrupts absolutely." The people of India experienced this at the hands of the Moghul rulers. Some of them became ruthless, even though they were very pious in their personal lives. The attachment and fervor for religion can also create havoc; Emperor Aurangzeb was the prime example. He was religiously very pious, yet he killed his brothers and imprisoned his father to become the Emperor of India. During his time, Guru Nanak Dev ji's tenth manifestation, Sri Guru Gobind Singh ji appeared on the scene to present a Sant Sipahi (the Spiritual Warrior) model of integration of spiritual and temporal power, which impacts every householder's life. This is the climactic story of Sri Guru Gobind Singh ji, the tenth and last human manifestation of Guru Nanak Dev ji as The Guru.

Bachitar Natak (A Mysterious Play)

Sri Guru Gobind Singh ji described his life in his autobiographical ballad Bachitar Natak (a mysterious play). It covers the period from his birth in 1666 until just before the manifestation of Khalsa, the pure one in 1699.

It is mainly written in *Bir Ras* (heroic poetry). The Indian arts and literature have nine main Rasaas (emotional pleasure or enjoyment of emotional states of mind): love, mirth, pity, anger, heroism, terror, hate, wonder, and contentment.

Bir Ras ballads evoke the emotions of chivalry, bravery and courage. To infuse this spirit among the Sikhs, Guru Gobind Sing ji chose to write his autobiography in this form. The rhythm, metaphors and images create a heightened sense of courage and bravery. The first part is an ode to *Kaal* (death) and *Akal* (Deathless, i.e., Waheguru the Creator). Bachitar Natak opens with the following Dohra (poetical form with two lines that rhyme):

Namaskar Sri kharag ko karousu hit chit laae

I salute the supreme Waheguru with all my love and heart.
Who holds all the power and the sword of Death.
This granth (book) will only be completed if You help me.

Tribhangi Chhand. (Praise of Death)

The power of sword (The death) cuts the evil people into pieces.
It destroys the armies in the battlefield.
This sword is indestructible.

It shines like the sun.

It brings power to the saints.

And destroys the evil persons.

It vanquishes all misdeeds.

I have taken shelter under such power.

O, the Power that Created this universe.

The whole world salutes Your victory.

You always protect me, victory be Yours.

Bhujhang Pryaat Chhand.

Waheguru is One Light. It does not go through

The cycle of birth and death.

It is the greatest of all gods and greatest of all kings.

It has no form, has no body, and no robes.

It is eternal.

It has all the powers and the Sword of Death.

I salute such a Being, who has all the powers.

Even though Waheguru is formless,

Yet It manifests in all the forms and moods.

Sometimes It is in *Rajas* state (power and activity),

At other times it is in a *Tamas* state (inertia, falsehood)

Other times, it is in a Satvik state (truth, reality).

Sometimes you are in a woman's form

Other times in a man's form

At times you are a Devi (female deity).

Other times you are a Deva (male deity).

Or may appear as a demon.

You manifest in great beautiful forms

Yet you are formless.

-Sri Dasam Granth Sahib ji, Bachitar Natak - P.148

In the first chapter, Guru Gobind Singh ji describes Waheguru's power and the power of different weapons, which are the manifestation of *Kaal* (death).

In the second chapter, Guru ji describes the history according to Hindu

Mythology. According to the epic, Ramayana, King Dasrath had four sons. Ram Chandar ji had two sons. Lav founded Lahore city and Kush founded Kasoor city. Lav's descendent, Kal Rai, defeated Kush's descendent, Kal Ket, and drove him out of Punjab. Along with his army, Kal Ket settled in Snaud. The king of Snaud gave his daughter in marriage to Kal Ket. He had a son called Sodhi Rai. When he began to rule Snaud, he decided to avenge his ancestor's defeat by invading Punjab, and he drove Lav's descendents out of Punjab.

Guru ji begins the third chapter by describing how Waheguru created great King Moh (attachment), and from whom no one can escape, and his great warriors Kaam (lust), Krodh (anger). Because of the attachments to worldly relatives and possessions, people get into conflicts. Then he describes the frightening battle between the descendents of Lav and Kush. Kal Rai's grandson Dev Rai was defeated and went to Kanshi (Banaras).

Chapter Four: Dev Rai studied Vedas in Kanshi, became famous and was respected for his piety and scholarship. Since they studied Vedas, they became known as Vedi (at present, they are known as Bedi). When the Raja of Sodhi family heard about the descendents of Lav becoming such pious scholars, he wrote to them and invited them back to Punjab. He said, since both of them had the same ancestors, they should forget their past enmity. Raja of Punjab listened to the Vedas. He was so influenced by the Vedic recitations and expositions that he gave up his Raj and went to the forest to live as a hemit. After the Vedis became the rulers of Punjab, they told the Sodhi Raja that in *Kalyug* (Dark Ages), the Vedi King would be born as Guru Nanak and the fourth Guru would be from the Sodhi family.

Chapter Five: In this chapter, Guru ji narrated the birth of Sri Guru Nanak

Dev ji. A long time before Guru Nanak was born, the Bedis had lost their Raj and they became farmers.

> In the family of Bedis manifested Nanak Rai,
> By Your grace brought peace to all the Sikhs.

Sri Guru Gobind Singh ji described the manifestation of Guru Nanak's Light in eight Gurus who succeeded him:

> Every one thought that the Gurus were different,
> Few recognized that it was the same manifestation.
> Those who recognized it, found the "way" (to truth or salvation).
> Others without understanding this could not grasp Reality.

Describing the ninth Guru Sri Guru Tegh Bahadur's martyrdom he wrote:

> He created a great event in *Kalyug* (Dark ages).
> He saved the Tilak and Janjoo (Sacred thread the Brahmins wear).
> For the sake of saints he sacrificed his life.
> He gave his head but did not even whisper a sigh.
> For the sake of Dharma, he created this great event
> He gave his head,
> But did not relinquish his faith and determination.
> Did not indulge in miracles or magical performance.
> Devotees of the Beloved, feel ashamed of such performances.[2]
> At the demise of Tegh Bahadur (Martyrdom)
> There prevailed a great sadness in the world.
> There were cries of lamentation in the world.
> But there were celebrations of victory,
> In the land of spiritual beings.

In Chapter Six, Sri Guru Gobind Singh begins the story of his life. Before

---

[2]The Sikh Gurus consider performing miracles as interference in Waheguru's Bhana. Aurangzeb wanted him to perform miracles and Guru Tegh Bahadur refused. Sri Ram Rai performed miracles and he was vanquished. (see page 143,148)

he was born, he meditated on Hemkunt Mountain with a lake surrounded by seven peaks. At the turn of the century, a retired army Sikh discovered this place. Now there is a Gurdwara Hemkunt Sahib at about 15,000 ft. above sea level. To reach there, you go through Hardawar and Rishikesh. Guru ji wrote:

> I meditated in such a way,
> From two I became One (merged with the Beloved).
> My parents were completely absorbed in meditation of the Supreme,
> They practiced all kinds of Jog and Sadhna (meditation)
> Because they were so devoted to the Infinite.
> The greatest Guru Dev (Enlightener Creator) blessed them.
> And I was born in *Kalyug* (Dark Age).
> I did not want to come.
> My consciousness was completely absorbed in the Beloved,
> The Supreme Being convinced me and sent me
> Into this world with these words:
> The Waheguru narrated to me how the Creator created powerful demons.
> They became so proud of their power
> And began to exercise their power,
> And wanted people to worship them.
> Then, Waheguru created gods, Rishis, Munis, Sidhas, Yogis
> And other great prophets.
> They all began to call themselves God
> And wanted people to worship them.
> Then the Akal Purkh said to me,

Words of the Eternal, Chaopai:

> I establish you as my son.
> I have created you to start a Panth.
> Everywhere spread Dharma.
> Stop people from foolish deeds.
>   *Kab-bach Dohra*

163

I stood with folded hands and head bowed down and said
That such True Panth can only be started with your support.

Guru ji stated that he came to abide by *Akal Puarkh*'s orders; he did not
come to have enmity with anyone:

Anyone who calls me *Parmeshwar* (God) would
Suffer in *Narak Kund* (Place of suffering or hell).
Consider me a servant of the Supreme.
Don't entertain any other consideration.

Guru ji added:

I am the servant of the Perfect Being.
I have come to see the play of this world.
I am going to give the message the Beloved has given me.
I will not be quiet because of fear of anyone in this world.
Whatever the Beloved has said to me
I am saying to the World.
Whosoever meditates on the Beloved
Goes to Swarag at the end.
Waheguru and the devotee are the same.
There is no difference between them.
As the wave springs up from water.
And merges back into it.

In Chapter Seven, Guru ji described his birth in Patna Sahib, his childhood
there and return to Anandpur Sahib.

In Chapter Eight, Guru ji describes the great battle of Bhangani when
Pahari Rajas attacked him. After defeating their combined forces, he returned to Anandpur Sahib.

In Chapter Nine, Guru ji describes the battle of Nadauon against the two generals of the Lahore Governor of Emperor Aurangzeb who came to collect revenue from the Pahari Raja Bhim Chand who had invaded Guru Sahib at Bhangani. Pahari Raja Bhim asked for Guru ji's help. Guru ji helped him to defeat the Moghul Generals.

Chapter Ten: A brief battle near Anandpur Sahib, in which Khanzada of Lahore retreated.

Chapter Eleven: Describes the Husaini's intentions to invade Anandpur Sahib.

Chapter Twelve: Describes the battle of Rustam Khan.

Chapter Thirteen: Describes the march of Shahzada Muazam Khan (Prince Bahadur Shah) through Anandpur Sahib.

Chapter Fourteen: In the last chapter, Guru ji thanks Waheguru. Because of Akal Purakh, he was victorious and protected against all evil designs. Anyone who is devoted to Waheguru receives Its protection.

The above incidents will be discussed in a chronological sequence in Guru ji's life. The first seven chapters describe in his own words how Guru Gobind Singh was sent to this world to continue to show the true path of loving devotion to Sat Naam (True Name) of One Creator, stated by Guru Nanak. He came to liberate people from the religious oppression of superstition, hypocritical, ritualistic practices and to make people aware of the Unity in diversity. He was the Dusht Daman (the destroyer of the cruel, evil minded oppressors). He had to organize a Panth, who would protect those who have no other protection, fight against injustice from anyone. In the following pages, an attempt is made to briefly narrate the life story of Guru Gobind Singh ji, and how Waheguru protected him while he was carrying out Akal Purakh's orders.

Guru Gobind Singh Ji's Birth

Sri Guru Gobind Singh ji was born in Patna, the capital of Bihar on December 22, 1666. His mother was Mata Gujri ji, and his father was Sri Guru Tegh Bahadur ji. He was named Gobind Rai.

A Muslim saint, Faqir Bhikhan Shah ji, lived in the village of Ghram. Originally from a village in Ambala District, he was highly respected and had a great following, judged from the size of the Masjid (mosque) that still exists. The day Guru Gobind Singh ji was born, he performed his Namaz (prayers) facing East instead of the West toward Mecca. His followers asked him about such a strange act.

He told them that God's manifestation had appeared in Patna. He travelled to Patna and reached there in one month and 20 days. When Faqir Bhikhan Shah ji reached there, Guru Tegh Bhadur ji had not returned home from Brahmputra, Assam. Guru Gobind Singh ji's mother and Maama (maternal uncle) Kirpal ji were very protective of the child, and did not want to expose him to strangers. He was their only child. When he was born his parents were married for approximately 29 years. They agreed to let Faqir ji see the child, who had brought two containers of sweets. He offered these to the child to see which one he would prefer. The child put his hands on both of them and smiled. Faqir Bhikhan Shah ji's followers asked him the meaning of this event. Pir Bhikhan Shah explained that he bought one container of sweets from a Muslim confectioner and the other from a Hindu. He wanted to find out which community he would prefer to guide and protect when he became the Guru. Since he put his hands on both the containers, he would love them equally.

166

Return To Anandpur Sahib

Guru Tegh Bahadur ji returned to Punjab when Gobind Rai was 7 years old. He bought a piece of land in Anandpur Sahib in Bilaspur State, ruled by Raja Bhim Chand. At the time, this hill was heavily wooded, and people were afraid to go there. There were superstitions that demons and evil spirits haunted the forested hills. Soon after Guru ji settled there, it became a place of pilgrimage. The Guru's Sikhs came from all over India to join the Sadh Sangat (companionship of the saints) and receive spiritual guidance and instructions from Guru ji.

When Gobind Rai ji was only nine years old, a delegation of Brahmins came to visit his father, Sri Guru Tegh Bahadur Sahib, at Anandpur Sahib because of the atrocities heaved upon them by Emperor Aurangzeb.

The story of Guru Tegh Bahadur Sahib's martyrdom is narrated on pages 153-155. Guru ji knew from experience that just after fifth Gurus ji's Martyrdom, his successor son Sri Guru Hargobind Sahib was imprisoned in Gwaliar fort when he was 17. Moreover, Guru Gobind Singh ji came to this world with specific instructions to protect the saints and the oppressed, and destroy oppression and evil. Therefore, he began the construction of three forts in Anandpur Sahib. He sent messages to Sikhs all over India, that they should bring horses and weapons when they came to visit him. He began imparting martial instructions to make his Sikhs warriors. He commissioned to construct a huge drum *Ranjeet Nagara* (victory drum), and when it was completed, its sound resounded throughout the hills and valleys.

The *Pahari Rajas* (the Rajas of the mountain ranges of Himachal Pradesh, and some parts of Uttar Pradesh) began to fear him. Guru Sahib met with them in Raval Sar near Mandi to tell them that he had no material ambition. He was not preparing to invade anyone. He was preparing to

167

defend the oppressed against the cruel oppressive regime of Aurangzeb. He asked them to join him, **but They refused. They objected to his Practice of equality, where everyone was welcome to join regardless of one's caste, creed, gender, status or vocation. They felt it was insulting for them as Kashatryas and Rajas to sit as equals in Sangat and Pangat. They continued to be suspicious and resentful.**

While Guru Teg Bahadur Sahib was in Patna, Raja Ram Rai of Assam and his Rani came to visit him because they had no children. After they asked Guru ji's blessings, a son was born to them. They named him Ratan Rai. He was born at almost the same time that Sri Guru Gobind Singh ji was born. Raja Ratan Rai decided to pay his regards to the Guru Ghar (house of the Guru). He came to Anandpur Sahib with six very expensive gifts costing Rs 125,000.00 each: A *Kalghi* (plume studded with precious stones), which Sri Guru Gobind Singh ji wore on his turban, an elephant that could perform several acts of service to Guru ji, a weapon with five weapons built into it (*Panj Kala Shastar*), a bejeweled cushioned throne, five horses with gold trappings, and a costly cup to drink water and milk. Raja Ratan Rai requested that these gifts be brought for Guru ji with his deepest love and regard. He beseeched Guru ji that these gifts were for his exclusive use and he would not allow anyone else to use them.

Raja Bhim Chand of Bilaspur made arrangements for his son Ajmer Chand's engagement to the daughter of Raja Fatah Shah of Sri Nagar, Garwhal. He sent his envoy to borrow Guru Sahib's elephant, Kabuli Shamyana (a large canopy tent) and the Panj Kala weapon to be exhibited during his son's engagement as a sign of his glory. In those days, many Rajas treated their subjects and their possessions as their own property. Nevertheless, Guru Sahib refused to loan the gifts. This angered Raja Bhim Chand. He wanted to invade Anandpur Sahib, but his advisors prevailed upon him. They told him that Guru Sahib also had an army, and would fight and kill many people. It was not a good omen just before the engagement of his son. Raja Bhim Chand gulped his pride, but never forgot this insult as he perceived it.

Paunta Sahib and Battle of Bhangani

Meantime, the Raja Medani Chand at Nahan invited Guru Sahib to spend some time with him, and Guru Sahib agreed. A small fortress was built for Guru Sahib and his Sikhs in Paunta. Now there is a Gurdwara Paunta Sahib, not far from Dehradoon. Guru Sahib's usual routine was to wake up three hours before sunrise, bathe, do his Paath and Simran, take a walk along Jamna river, find a place of solitude to contemplate, and write poetry for three hours.

Sikhs started flocking around him. There was a Pathan Pir Budhu Shah, a highly regarded spiritual guide among Muslims. His sister was married to Daler Khan, one of the Generals of Aurangzeb. He lived in Sadhaur with his several hundred followers. Five hundred soldiers from Moghul army deserted and went to Pir Budhu Shah. He sent them to Guru Sahib who accepted them in his service. An Udasi Mahant Kirpal also joined Guru Sahib with his 400 followers. Raja of Nahan had a border land dispute with the neighboring Raja Fatah Shah of Sri Nagar; Guru Sahib brought them together and resolved their differences.

Then it came the time for Raja Bhim Chand's son, Ajmer Chand's wedding. The wedding party had to go by Paunta Sahib on their way to Sri Nagar. Because of his own resentment, Raja Bhim Chand did not want to face Guru Sahib, and went with his army and members of the wedding party to Sri Nagar by a different route. His son, Ajmer Chand, went to Guru ji. He paid his regards, bowed before Guru ji and said that he was like Guru ji's son and had come to ask for his blessings. Guru ji blessed him. He proceeded to Sri Nagar with his retinue.

The Raja of Sri Nagar Fatah Shah had a great regard for Guru Sahib and invited him to attend his daughter's wedding. Guru ji dispatched 500 of his Sikhs under the command of his Finance Minister Divan Nand Chand, with a *Shagan* (gifts & money given to bride or groom) of a necklace for his daughter worth Rs. 125,000.00. When Bhim Chand saw Divan Nand Chand present Guru Gobind Rai's gift in the presence of all the Pahari Rajas, he felt insulted and became enraged. He told Raja Fatah Shah, if he did not return Guru Sahib's gift, he would not let his son marry his daughter, and the wedding party would leave. This is considered the ultimate humiliation for the bride's parents. Raja Fatah Shah returned Guru Sahib's Shagan. Bhim Chand decided to annihilate the Sikhs who brought the Shagan. Guru Sahib had already cautioned them against the treachery of Pahari Rajas. Therefore, the Sikhs camped outside of the city. As soon as they discovered Raja Bhim Chand's plan, they escaped without injury or losses.

All the Rajas of 22 Pahari states were present at the wedding. Raja Bhim Chand thought this was a good opportunity for him to invite all the Rajas against Siri Guru Gobind Singh ji. He pointed out that Guru Sahib was away from Anandpur Sahib in a small fortress. It would be easy to crush his growing power once and for all. If they could arrest him alive, they could present him to Emperor Aurangzeb and receive a reward. Raja Fatah Shah still objected because Guru Sahib had always been his friend and the Raja had a great regard for him. He felt that it was petty to go to war because someone refused your request. It was sinful for a Rajput to go to war unprovoked. In Indian culture, the father of the bride is always in a one down position. Raja Bhim Chand again threatened that he would not accept his daughter as a daughter-in-law. Ultimately, all the Rajas agreed to attack Guru Sahib at Paunta Sahib.

When Guru Sahib heard about the intentions of the Pahari Rajas, he decided to meet them at Bhangani, about six miles from Paunta Sahib.

The 500 Pathans who deserted the Moghul army left Guru Sahib and joined the Pahari Rajas. They told the Pahari Rajas that Guru Sahib's soldiers were just a collection of riff raff. None of them was a professional soldier. If the Pahari Rajas would allow the Pathans to loot the Guru Sahib's treasuries and other possessions, they would fight on the side of the Pahari Rajas. On the Guru Sahib's side, the 400 followers of the Udassi Mahant sneaked away over night, but Mahant Kirpal stayed and begged Guru Sahib's forgiveness for his followers' conduct. Guru Sahib was left with just a few hundred loyal Sikhs.

Guru Sahib described this battle in the ballad of Bachitar Natak, Chapter nine. On both sides, the soldiers fought with great valor.

Guru Sahib directed the battle strategy from a small hilltop. When Guru Sahib arrived there, Bhai Daya Ram described the army position against him. Fatah Shah's army faced the Sikh positions and he was behind his army. On the right were 500 Pathans under the command of Haiyat Khan, Nijabat Khan and Bhikan Khan. Hari Chand, Raja of Handur, a great archer, was in a chariot heading his army. Raja Gopal of Guler, Raja of Chandel, Rajas of Dhalwal and Jasuwal and Cheif of Karori were specifically identified in Guru Sahib's description and how bravely they fought.

On Guru Sahib's side were his cousin Sango Shah, who fought with great valor near the end of the battle in which he was killed. Nijabat Khan and Sango Shah died while fighting with each other. When arrows and musket fire from both sides resounded through the hills, Pir Budhu Shah joined Guru Sahib with his four sons, two brothers and 700 disciples. The Udasi

Mahant approched Guru Sahib to join the battle. Guru Sahib told him he should pray for them because he spent all his life praying. Udassis renounced the world, let alone fighting; he persisted. Guru Sahib asked him, Which weapon would he use? Mahant Kirpal pointed to his metal club (gurj). Guru Sahib gave him a horse and blessed him. Udasis do not wear any clothes and have renounced the world. They are the followers of Guru Nanak Dev ji's son, Sri Chand.

Macauliffe (11) paraphrased Guru Sahib's description of the entry of Mahant Kirpal into the battle:

"...it was a spectacle to see the Mahant with his matted hair twisted round his head, his body only clothed with a thin plaster of ashes, and his belly projecting far in front of his saddle, proceeding to engage a practiced warrior armed with the latest weapons of destruction."

Mahant Kirpal rode directly to Pathan Haiyat Khan and challenged him. The Pathan walked away and did not want to fight him. Mahant kept taunting him until Haiyat Khan turned around in full fury and delivered a furious blow from his sword. The Mahant took it on his club. Then Mahant hit his head with his club. This cracked his skull, and Haiyat Khan fell dead. His club was wreaking havoc until the Pathans surrounded him. Guru Sahib sent his cousin, Jit Mal, who rained arrows on the Pathans and successfully rescued the Mahant.

A confectioner, Lal Chand, who had never held a sword in his hand, prayed to Guru Sahib to let him fight. Guru Sahib showed him how to hold a sword in his right hand and the shield in his left hand. He took Mir Khan's sword blow on his shield and finished him with one blow of his sword.

When Guru Sahib saw Sangu Shah fall, he called him Shah Sangram (the conqueror of battles), mounted his charger and galloped into battle. He engaged Hari Chand, the great archer, and let him shoot three arrows. The last one pierced Guru Sahib's belt, but did not injure him. Guru Sahib expressed his sorrow that Hari Chand was not taught well enough.

Guru Sahib released one arrow that struck Hari Chand dead. Seeing all their generals and Rajas dead or in flight, the armies fled and the Sikhs won their first battle against the transgressors. In the end Guru Sahib said that through the grace and protection of Waheguru the Sikhs were victorious.

Guru Sahib was doing what Waheguru instructed him to do. He felt that Waheguru's protective shield was always around him. Since he believed he was Waheguru's servant, the results belonged to Waheguru. He kept his Haumain out of it and he wanted the Sikhs also not to take credit for anything they did. This attitude is illustrated in the greeting which Guru Sahib proclaimed as the Sikh greeting:

Wahe Guru ji Ka Khalsa
Waheguru ji Ki Fateh

The Khalsa belongs to Waheguru
Victory is of Waheguru

Subsequently, Guru Sahib fought more then 14 battles. He never attacked anybody, but always rose to defend when attacked.

RETURN TO ANANDPUR SAHIB

After the defeat of Pahari Rajas at the battle of Bhangani, Guru Gobind Rai ji returned to Anandpur Sahib.

GURU, *THE BAKHASHAN HAAR* (FORGIVER)

As Sri Guru Gobind Singh stated in his autobiographical ballad "Bachitar Natak," he merged with Akal Purkh and became one with Akal Purkh. Therefore, he lived his life exhibiting all the attributes of Waheguru Akal Purkh. He had no enmity with anyone. Soon after he returned to Anandpur Sahib, the Moghul governor of Lahore, Dilawar Khan, sent Moghul General, Alaf Khan to collect Nazrana (a forced gift revenue) from the Pahari Rajas. Since Bhim Chand was the most prominent of them all, the Pahari Rajas told the Moghul General that if Bhim Chand would provide the demanded Nazrana, all the other Rajas would follow suit. Bhim Chand knew that he was no match against the Moghuls. He asked for Guru Sahib's help, and Guru Sahib obliged. Alif Khan was defeated in the battle of Nadaun. Bhim Chand thanked Guru Sahib and invited Guru Sahib to stay with him for a week so he could serve him. Guru Sahib returned to Anandpur Sahib after spending about eight days with Raja Bhim Chand.

THE CENTER OF LEARNING AND LITERATURE

Anandpur Sahib became a great place of literary creation. Sri Guru Gobind Rai had 52 poets, scholars and bards[1]. They composed poetry and translated stories from great Indian epics Ramayana, Mahabharta and Puranas into Braj Bhakha and Hindi, in ballad style and in Bir Ras. The purpose was to create a warrior spirit in the Sikhs and educate them in ancient classics. The Gurus emphasized the importance of learning and education. Guru Angad Dev ji perfected Gurmukhi script and started a school. Guru Gobind Singh ji sent his Sikhs to Banaras to acquire the knowledge of Vedas and ancient literature. Guru Sahib wrote in Punjabi, Sanskrit, Farsi, Hindi and Braj Bhakha. He wrote "Chandi Charitar", describing the great battle the Goddess Durga (kali) fought to reinstate the gods in Swarag Puri, the heavenly abode of the gods. The demons had turned them out of

---

[1] This is nominal number. In fact there were many more - many would come and go.

174

there and occupied it themselves. Goddess Durga helped the Gods to regain Swarag Puri. She destroyed the demons. At the end, there is the following epilogue of Goddess Durga praying to Akal Purkh. It has become the most popular Sikh prayer to remind us of our purpose:

deh shiva var mohe ihey

Oh, Powerful Creator give me this boon
That I should never shirk from doing good deeds.
Not have the slightest fear
Of engaging the enemy in the battle,
And with determined confidence be victorious.
I teach my mind the lesson
That I should always recite Your praises.
As my life comes to an end
I should die fighting in the battlefield.
          -Chandi Charitara Ukati Bilas, Dasam Granth - P.99

Foremost among this circle of poets was Bhai Nand Lal. Later, during his exodus from Anandpur Sahib, many of Guru Sahib's possessions were lost in the flooded Sirsa Nadi (a seasonal river). Most of the literature produced at Anandpur Sahib was also lost. After Guru Sahib's death, Bhai Mani Singh the head *Granthi* of Amritsar, compiled Dasam Granth (book of The Tenth Guru). There are quite a few questionable and controversial writings included in it. Some of these might have been written by the poets of Guru Sahib's entourage.

Nevertheless, there were quite a few authentic Guru Sahib's writings. His Jaap Sahib and Savaiye from, Akal Ustat are two of the five Banis (compositions of the Gurus) the Sikhs recite every morning.

GURU GOBIND SINGH. THE HOUSEHOLDER
Guru Gobind Singh ji had three wives - Mata Sundari ji, Mata Jito ji and Mata Sahib Devan ji. After the battle of Bhangani, Mata Sundari ji had

their first son in the month of *Magh*, year of Vikrami 1743 (1687 A.D.). Guru ji named him Ajit (unconquerable) Singh. The second son, Jhujar Singh, was born in the month of *Chet*, 1747. Zorawar Singh was born to his first wife Jito ji in the month of *Magh*, 1753 (1697 A.D.). The fourth and the youngest son, Fateh Singh, was born in the month of *Phagan*, 1755 (1699 A.D.)

Guru Sahib was very accessible to his Sikhs and their families. He respected their counsel. For example, the location for the battle of Bhangani was chosen by Bhai Daya Ram, and Guru Sahib accepted his suggestion.

Whenever the Sikhs were really concerned about something, they would go to his mother Mata Gujri ji. Guru Sahib loved and respected his mother. He would reason with her or demonstrate the validity of his decisions. He never brushed off any ideas or suggestions with the attitude that Guru knows better. For example, during the siege of Anandpur Sahib, the Sikhs approached Mata Gujri ji to request Guru Sahib to vacate the fort because the Pahari Rajas and the Moghuls had assured a safe passage. Instead of arguing, he told them to wait until night. He asked the Sikhs to load a bunch of bullock carts with all the garbage in Anandpur Sahib. He covered all of it with shiny silk and brocade, and walked them out of the fort as a caravan. As soon as these carts came out of the fort gates, the *Pahari Rajas'* armies attacked them. Thus, they realized Guru ji's decision was wise.

One day, Mata Jito ji went to Guru Sahib and told him that she saw in her meditation that her sons were being killed. She beseeched Guru Sahib to avert this fate because he had spiritual powers. Guru Sahib told her that he had also known this. Nevertheless, this is Waheguru's Bhana, and one should not interfere with Akal Purkha's design; instead, one should abide by Its Will.

He experienced all the joys of being a son, father and a husband and the suffering that comes through their losses, yet he always accepted Waheguru's Bhana. He sent his father, Sri Guru Tegh bahadur ji, for Martyrdom when he was only nine years old. As we will see, he sacrificed his four sons, his mother and ultimately his own life, but never for a second deterred from the task assigned to him, i.e. to love and meditate on one Creator's Name (Naam Simran), protect the saints and oppressed, and destroy the evil and cruel oppressors. Guru Sahib adored his sons. He personally trained them to meditate and do Simran; he trained *them* as warriors.

THE MANIFESTATION OF THE KHALSA

khalsa akal purkh ki fauj

Khalsa Is Akal Purkh' s (The Eternal Being) Army
Khalsa Manifested By the Pleasure of Parmatma (Supreme Soul))
-Sarabloh Granth, (15) Vol. 2 - P.532

By 1699, Sri Guru Gobind Rai ji had infused the warrior spirit into the Sikhs. Since the time of Sri Guru Nanak Dev ji, the Sikhs learned to live in Waheguru consciousness as householders. He liberated them from the tyranny of hypocritical Brahmanical practices, the oppression of the caste system, and oppressive social customs. Guru Gobind Rai imparted martial training to the Sikhs and taught them how to be fearless **(Nirbhao)** in fighting against tyranny and oppression. They experienced this in the battle of Bhangani. He taught them to have no enmity **(Nirvair)** with anyone. They experienced it in the battle of Nadaun in which Guru Sahib accepted the prayer of Pahari Rajas to protect them against the Moghul army led by Husaini. Guru Sahib led them to victory. The same Pahari Rajas who had attacked him at Bhanagani to annihilate him and his Sikhs. **His battles were not motivated by political ambitions against any person. They were to protect the poor, vulnerable and oppressed people against the tyranny of the unjust, fanatic rulers.**

In his autobiographical ballad of Bachitar Natak Guru Sahib mentioned that through deep meditation he "became One from two." He had merged with the Akal Purkh. The time had come to merge the Sikhs with Akal Purkh and become Akal Moorat **(The manifestation of the Eternal)**. Guru Gobind Singh had become the servant of Waheguru and fought for Dharma, fearlessly recited Naam, and prevented people from getting distracted from Waheguru by the great "King Haumain." Now was the time to organize the Sikhs to such a Panth (organized community) and abide by the orders of the Akal Purkh. The highest virtue of being a Sikh is to do selfless Sewa (service). Now they were ready to learn to offer the ultimate sacrifice of their own life in the service of humanity. **When a Sikh fights for any material gain or personal vested interest, then he/she is not a part of the Akal Purkh's Fauj. He/she is not a Khalsa.**

Macauliffe (11) gives the following account of the creation of Khalsa;

Guru Gobind Rai sent messages across India to all the Sikhs that on Baisakhi day of March 30, 1699, he was going to bless the Sikhs with a special boon he prepared for them. The Pahari Rajas and the Moghul administration tried to prevent the Sikhs from reaching Anandpur Sahib. Three hundred years ago, there were no fast transportation means. In spite of all the obstructions and travel difficulties, 80,000 Sikhs reached Siri Anandpur Sahib from all parts of India.

After the Kirtan of Asa Di Var, Sri Guru Gobind Rai drew his sword and asked if anyone in the Sangat was willing to sacrifice himself. There was complete silence. At last, one out of 80,000 people came forward and said that he had already surrendered himself to the Guru the day he became his Sikh. His life belonged to the Guru ever since. Therefore, it is already Guru's, so the Guru could do with it whatever he wished. His name was Bhai Daya Ram. Guru ji took him in the nearby enclosed tent, and people heard the sound of a thud. He came out with a blood-drenched sword, and demanded the sacrifice of one more Sikh. He repeated this demand five times. In this manner, the following five persons came forward:

1. Bhai Daya Ram a Khatri from Lahore
    son of Sudha ji and Diali ji
2. Bhai Dharam Das, a Jat from Hastinapur (Delhi),
    son of Sant Ram ji and Sabho ji.
3. Bhai Mohkam Chand, a washerman from Dwarka,
    son of Tirath Ram ji and Devanbai ji.
4. Bhai Sahib Chand, a barber from Bidar,
    son of Chanmaji and Sonabai ji.
5. Bhai Himmat Rai, a jheevar (water carrier) from Jagannath
    Puri, He was the son of Gulzari ji and Dhanno ji.

It is noteworthy that these five people came from five different parts of India and belonged to different castes. He brought these five Sikhs out of the tent dressed in shorts up to the knee and new blue robes, saffron turbans and swords.

Guru Gobind Rai ji poured water into a large steel bowl (*Bata*). Mata Jito ji poured sugar chips (*Patasch*) into the bowl. Guru ji meditated and recited the following Banis as he stirred the Patasch in the water with a double edged sword (Khanda);

1. Japji Sahib
2. Jaap Sahib
3. Anand Sahib
4. Savaiye (From Guru Gobind Singh's Bani Akal Ustat)

After he finished his recitation meditation, he went to each of the five and asked them to say Waheguru and recite the Mool Mantar from Jap ji Sahib. After each recitation, he gave them one palmful of Amrit to drink. This way, he gave each of them five palmfuls of Amrit to drink. He sprinkled it five times on their hair, five times on their eyes, and asked them to repeat Waheguru ji Ka Khalsa, Waheguru ji Ki Fateh. He gave them the last name of Singh, which means a lion. They were asked to wear the following, each of which begins with the letter K. *Kes* (Unshorn hair), *Kangha* (comb), *Kirpan* (Sword), *Kach* (Shorts), *Kara* (A steel bracelet). Their former caste was erased. They became the warriors of Akal Purkh's army and the *Amrit* (Nector of eternity) made them merge with the Akal while they were still living in their body, but were not attached to it. They became the Khalsa, the pure ones. They became *Amritdhari* Sikhs, i.e., they incorporated nectar of eternity, which was created from Naam. Akal Purkh had transformed them into spiritual warriors.

amrit naam nidhan hai mil peevo bhai

Naam is the supreme Nector of Eternity
Brothers get together and drink it.
-Guru Arjan Dev ji, SGGS - P.318

After he blessed the Panj Payare (The Beloved Five) with Amrit, Guru Gobind Rai kneeled before the five to bless him with the same boon of Amrit. One of the Panj Payare asked Guru Sahib "We had offered the sacrifice of our life, what is your offering". Guru Gobind Rai ji replied that he would offer the sacrifice of his whole family. He had already sacrificed his father. Later on his mother and four sons, and ultimately himself was sacrificed serving the Akal Purkh and Its Creation. This is why Guru Sahib is called Sarbans Dani (who gave the offering of his family). The Panj Payare performed the same ceremony of Amrit blessing and Guru Gobind Rai was also transformed into Gobind Singh.

vah pragteo mard agamra varyam akela

There manifested a matchless brave warrior
who has no equal.
Praise Guru Gobind Singh,
who himself is the Guru and the Disciple.

-Varan Bhai Gurdas - Var 1/17

This is in keeping with the essence of Sikh practice. Waheguru and the Sikh are the same, only our Haumain creates the separation. Lehna ji became Angad, a manifestation of Guru Nanak. The fourth Guru wrote about Waheguru;

apey gur chela hai apey

" It is Itself the Guru itself the Sikh."

-Guru Ram Das ji, SGGS - P.669

Guru Gobind Singh declared that his Sikhs would be as sweet as mother's love (Pataseh from Mata Jito ji) and they will be strong like the Khanda when fighting oppression. Through meditation Naam Simran, they will stay attached to Akal Purkh and detached from Haumain.

Guru ji attributed all his successes to his Sikhs. He thanked them, rather he said without them he would not have any significance. It is clear from his writing below translated by Macauliffe (11):

yudh jite inhee key prasaad

My victories in battle have been through their favor;
Through their favor I have made gifts of charity,
Through their favor all my troubles have been removed;
Through their favor again my house is replenished;
Through their favor I have acquired knowledge;
Through their kindness all the enemies have been destroyed,

Through their favor I am exalted.
Otherwise there are millions of poor men like myself.
-Dasam Granth (Khalsa Mahima) - P.716-717

Guru Gobind Singh told us in Bachitar Natak that he was only carrying out the orders of Akal Purkh. Therefore, It always protected him. Since it was Waheguru's bidding, all the success was Waheguru's blessing. To protect Sikhs from the strong shackles of "Haumain King", Guru Sahib wanted them to remember who they really were, and whatever they achieved was not because of them, therefore, he incorporated it in the Sikh greeting as well as the salutation at the end of all recitations and meditation.

Waheguru ji Ka Khalsa
Waheguru Ji Ki Fateh!

The Khalsa belongs to Waheguru
The Victory belongs to Waheguru!

There were great warriors in human history. Most of them fought for personal, sectarian, religious or temporal power. **Guru Gobind Singh and the Khalsa are non-sectarian. The Khalsa fights only to protect the saints, the unprotected and oppressed against injustice and tyranny of the powerful. As soon as a person in the name of Khalsa, fights** for **any temporal or sectarian gain, he/she ceases to be Khalsa.**

gur sangat keeni khalsa

The Khalsa emerged from Guru Sangat;
That Guru Sangat that was created
By Baba Nanak with dedication to Naam.

Sadh Sangat:

sat sangat kaisi janiey, jithai eko naam vakhanie

Consider *Sat Sangat* the one
where there is only the meditation on Naam.
-Guru Nanak Dev ji, SGGS - P.72

Through such meditation, a person becomes one with Waheguru and ultimately gets the courage to become a Sant Sipahi (Spiritual Warrior), the Khalsa. He/She selflessly serves the Akal Purkh and Its creation.

The spiritual warrior's first and foremost battle is to conquer Man (mind) that is pulled by Haumain to pursue lust, anger, greed, attachment and pride.

jo jan loojeh manai sio

> The person who battles with the mind is the supreme warrior
> The one who is merged with the Divine
> And has recognized his true nature
>
> -SGGS - P.1089

Unfortunately, the Sikh leadership in recent years has been possessed by "Haumain King" and has become quite sectarian and egotistical. We have even added to Ardas in some Gurdwaras, "Bless the Panth with it's own Raj Bhag." Our Guru says,

**raj na chahoon, mukt naa chahoon
chahoon preet charan kamala Re**

> I do not want **Raj** or **Mukti**,
> I only desire the Love of Your Lotus Feet.
>
> -Guru Arjan Dev ji, SGGS - P.534

Furthermore, Khalsa, the spiritual warrior lives by the following:

mat hondi hoe ianaa

> Having intellectual prowess maintains his innocence,
> Having strength, he is humble,
> He shares beyond what he has,
> Such a person can be called a Bhagat.
>
> -Bhai Gurdas ji

183

The Khalsa serves Waheguru, no matter what his/her worldly role is, whether one is a poor laborer, a C.E.O. of a multinational corporation, or a president or prime minister of a country. As long as one is connected to Akal Purkh and serves all humanity equally, one is living like a Khalsa. The name and form of oppressor changes. One should not identify with the oppressor, but always be on the side of the oppressed. For example, currently the oppressors are the greedy multinational corporations (8) functioning in collaboration with the power elite of every country with I.M.F. (3) and the World Bank as their instruments. They are the instruments to satiate unbridled greed. They insist on restructuring the economy and destroying all social and human service programs. You have to identify the oppressor before you can lift the oppression. If we are blessed to be a member of the power elite i.e., a part of the educational, religious, media, business, political power, we should try to be socially responsible and spiritually enlightened.

We may need to use different weapons, such as education and forging the anti-oppressive alliances. Helping the power elite to get in touch with their True Divine identity and develop peaceful ways of conflict resolution.

Code of Conduct
Guru Gobind Singh ji also gave the following code of conduct for the Khalsa that includes already existing Gurbani simran (14).

First and foremost is Nitnem (Daily Practice); getting up before sunrise. After bath, meditation on Naam, then reciting Japji Sahib, Jaap Sahib, Anand Sahib and Savaiye of tenth Guru. This is preparation for starting the day. In the evening, recite Rehras Sahib to wash out the impact of Haumain-based Karmic world. Recite Kirtan Sohila before going to sleep to remember the impermanent nature of this life and merge with the Akal Purkh.

Macauliffe described the Muktnama (The epistle of salvation) in vols. V and VI page 116 as advice to the two Sikhs who were quarreling over a debt. It is very close to Rehatnama, the code of conduct.

The Guru repeated for the first time his 'Muktnamas', or means of salvation. The following are its principal injunctions: '0 Sikhs, borrow not, but, if you are compelled to borrow faithfully restore the debt. Speak not falsely and associate not with the untruthful. Associating with holy men, practice truth, love truth, and clasp it to your hearts. Live by honest labor and deceive no one. Let not a Sikh be covetous. Repeat the Jap ji and the Jaap ji before eating. Look not on a naked woman. Let not your thoughts turn towards that sex. Cohabit not with another's wife. Deem another's property as filth. Keep your bodies clean. Have dealings with everyone, but consider yourselves distinct. Your faith and daily duties are different from theirs. Bathe every morning before repast. If your bodies endure not cold water, then heat it. Ever abstain from tobacco and all intoxicants, such as, alcohol or opium. Remember the one immortal God. Repeat the Rahiras in the evening and the Sohila at bedtime. Receive the Amrit and teaching of the Guru, and act according to the Granth Sahib. Cling to the boat in which thou has embarked. Wander not in search of another religion. Repeat the Guru's hymns day and night. Marry only into the house of a Sikh. Preserve thy wife and thy children from evil company. Covet not money offered for religious purposes. Habitually attend a Sikh temple and eat a little Langar, the sacred food from there. He who distributeth sacred food should do so in equal quantities, whether the recipients be high or low, old or young. Eat not food offered to gods or goddesses. Despise not any Sikh, and never address him without the appellation, "Singh". Eat regardless of caste with all Sikhs who have had Amrit, and deem them your brethren. Abandon at once the company of Brahmans and Mullas who cheat men out of their wealth, of ritualists who lead Sikhs astray, and of those who give women in marriage with concealed physical defects, and thus deceive the hopes of off spring.

' Let not a Sikh have intercourse with a strange woman unless married to her according to the Sikh rites. Let him contribute a tenth part of his earnings for religious purposes. Let him bow down at the conclusion of prayer. When a Sikh die, let sacred food, Langar, be prepared. After his cremation let the Sohila be read and prayer offered for his soul and for the consolation of his relations. Then sacred food may be distributed. Let not the family of the deceased indulge in much mourning, or bevies of women join in lamentation. On such occasions let the Gurus' hymns be read and sung, and let all listen to them.

"Worship not an idol, and drink not the water in which it has been bathed. The rules of caste and of the stages of Hindu life are erroneous. Let my Sikhs take care not to practice them. 0 Sikhs, listen to me and adopt not the ceremonies of the Hindus for the supposed advantages of the manes of ancestors.

' My face is turned towards him who calleth out to a Sikh "Waheguru ji ki Fateh"' my right shoulder towards him who returneth the salutation with love, my left shoulder towards him who retumeth it as a matter of custom, and my back towards him who retumeth it not at all. To him who abideth by these rules I will grant a position to which no one as yet been able to attain, and which was beyond the conception of Shankar Acharya, Dattatre, Ramanuj, Gorakh, and Muhammad.

'As, when rain falleth on the earth, the fields yield excellent and pleasant fruit, so he who listeneth to the Guru and attendeth to all these injunctions shall assuredly receive the reward thereof. Whoever accepteth the Guru's words, and these rules which he had given, shall have his sins pardoned; he shall be saved from transmigration through the eighty-four lakhs of animal births, and after death shall enter the Guru's abode. If any worldly man devoted to pleasure tell you to the contrary, listen not to him, but ever follow the Guru's instruction'.

(Macauliffe, Vol. V. p. 116-119)

By the later researcher this Mukatnama is not considered authentic. Dr. Bhai Sahib Singh's Mukatnama in Sakhi - 8 of his book, Sau Sakhi, is considered more authentic (13).

Thus came into being the Khalsa Panth of Spiritual Warriors, who maintain their distinctness and detachment from Haumain, dedicated to the service of Waheguru and it's Creation.

As long as the Khalsa maintains its distinct identity
I will give Khalsa all the Light and strength
When Khalsa follows Brahmanical rituals
Then I will not be with them.

Approximately, 20,000 Sikhs became Amritdhari Khalsa during the Baisakhi week.

A Year Of Peace

People from all over India became aware of the way of life of equality, meditation on Naam, being kind and serving humanity. If anyone was cruel to them, they came to Guru Sahib for help.

Restoring Brahmin's Wife: One night, a young Brahmin came to Guru Sahib and told him that some soldiers had abducted his wife. Guru Sahib's eldest son, Sahibzada Ajit Singh, volunteered to go on the rescue mission. He took a small jatha (a group) of Khalsa warriors. By morning, he brought back the Brahmin's wife, arrested the perpetrators, and they were admonished never ever even to attempt such a heinous act.

Bibi Dip Kaur: It was not unusual for the Moghul soldiers to harass or torture Sikhs; therefore, they usually traveled in groups. Once a group of Majha Sikhs (from Lahore and Amritsar Districts) were travelling to Anandpur Sahib to visit Sri Guru Gobind Singh ji. The jatha stopped at a well to rest under a shady tree and get some water. Bibi Dip Kaur continued riding on her horse. She had not gone far, when a group of four Moghuls, thinking, she was alone young woman, surrounded her. Bibi Dip Kaur threw down her gold bracelet. When one of them stooped down to grab the bracelet, and Bibi Dip Kaur chopped off his head. The other three were stunned. They did not expect an innocent woman to be

187

trained in martial arts. Before they could regain their senses, they met the same fate. Meanwhile the other members of the jatha arrived and joined her. When they arrived at Anandpur Sahib, they told the heroic story of Bibi Dip Kaur, Guru Sahib blessed her, and **admired her for her courage, presence of mind and skill.**

There are innumerable stories of Sikh courage and defiance in the face of great odds. There is a slogan they lived by, "Khalsa is ever tayar bar tayar" (Ever Prepared). Guru Sahib's instruction that Khalsa should develop martial skills and always be armed, was useful one.

Hola Mohalla:

During the Indian festival of Holi, people spray color on each other. (Most people do not remember the historical significance of the festival.) In Anandpur Sahib, Guru Sahib replaced it with a festival of martial arts and warfare, in which warriors display their martial skills and war strategies. They called it Hola Mohalla. Once, a Brahmin commented how Sikhs could be spiritual, enjoy all the pleasures of life, and eat meat. Guru Sahib replied that the Sikhs always meditate on Akal Purkh and enjoy life's pleasures with Its blessing. Another time, Madho Nath Jogi said, "how could you be a holy man wearing this royal attire and jewel studded plume on your turban? You indulge in worldly glory." The Guru replied, "These royal robes are to scare the cruel Turks, faqiri is within me."

Breach of Faith By Pahari Rajas

The Brahmins were against the Sikhs for abolishing the caste system, thus depriving them of their elitist position and financial gains by exploiting people with their superstitious religious practices. The Pahari Rajas not only felt threatened by the growing Sikh power, they felt demeaned that non-Rajputs and non-Kashatris (these were the warrior and ruling castes) were treated equal to low castes and were trained as warriors of Khalsa.

The Rajas had already suffered defeats at the hands of the Sikh warriors. Now, the formal establishment of a Khalsa Panth was very hard for them to take. The Raja of Bilaspur asked Guru Gobind Singh to pay rent to him for use of his state land. Guru Sahib reminded him that his father, Guru Tegh Bahadur, bought this land when it was nothing but forested hill; therefore, he refused to pay rent. This was just an excuse to get rid of Guru ji and his Khalsa.

The combined forces of Pahari Rajas attacked Anandpur Sahib several times, but the Khalsa repelled the attacks.

Pahari Rajas realized that they could not alone defeat the Khalsa army, and approached the Moghul Governor of Sarhind province. Moghuls were as apprehensive of the Khalsa as the Pahari Rajas. Wazir Khan, the Governor of Sarhind, dispatched an army of 10,000 soldiers under the command of Din Beg and Painde Khan. They joined 20,000 soldiers of combined Pahari Raja forces. The Pahari Rajas also asked their Muslim subjects Ranghars and Gujars to join them. Guru Sahib had a total of 7,000 Khalsa in all three forts. One gate of the fort was defended by Bhai Daya Singh, the second by Alam Singh, and the third one by Guru Sahib's son, Sahibzada Ajit Singh. Commander Painde Khan advanced and challenged Guru Gobind Singh and asked him to strike the first blow. Guru ji told him he never did that. Painde Khan shot two arrows and missed. Painde Khan was completely covered with metallic armor, except his ears. Guru Sahib shot an arrow that pierced through his ears, and he fell dead. Din Beg was wounded and fled from the battlefield.

Realizing they could not defeat the Khalsa in an open battle, they decided to blockade all supplies coming into the fort. This went on for two months. Then they thought of another scheme. They intoxicated an elephant covered with steel armor and a spear projecting from his forehead, and let him loose before the gate of the fort. The elephant was severely injured by Bachitar Singh, turned around and trampled his own army.

The Pahari Rajas hired two Muslim brothers to assassinate the Guru with their heavy guns. One evening, Guru Sahib was fired upon, and one of his attendants was killed. Guru Sahib took his bow and shot a gold-tipped arrow that struck the gunman down. Guru Sahib used the gold tipped arrows so that survivors of the soldier's family could have arranged a respectable funeral. Poor soldiers fight for ambitious rulers in order to earn a livelihood. Guru ji had to defend himself, but did not consider anyone an enemy. The arrow struck the gunner before he could reload the gun, and he was killed. His brother came forward to load the gun, and he met the same fate by Guru Sahib's arrow.

Finally, the Pahari Rajas wrote him a letter of regret requesting him to help them to save face. If he vacated the fort and accepted the invitation of the Raja of Basoli, they could claim that they succeeded in having Guru Sahib vacate the Anandpur Sahib fort. Guru Sahib accepted the invitation. He stayed in Basoli for a couple of months, then returned to Anandpur Sahib. The residents gave him a tumultuous welcome because they had missed his presence.

The Exodus From Anandpur Sahib

Emperor Aurangzeb was quite perturbed by the defeat of Royal armies sent by the Governor of Sarhind under the command of Painde Khan and Din Beg. The envoy soldier from Sarhind explained that the Sikhs attacked them totally unaware. Aurangzeb asked him to describe what kind of a man Guru Gobind Singh was, and how big an army he had. The Muhammadan soldier gave highly colorful accounts of the Guru's beauty, sanctity, and prowess.

"He was, he said, a young handsome man, living saint, the father of his people, and in war equal to one hundred thousand men."

(Macauliff, Vol. V, p. 164)

This infuriated Emperor Aurangzeb and he ordered the soldier to be taken out of his sight. The Emperor sent Guru Sahib the following message:

"There is only one Emperor. Thy religion and mine are the same. Come to see me by all means, otherwise I shall be angry and go to thee. If thou come, thou shalt be treated as holy men are treated by monarchs". (11)

Guru ji was well aware of the treachery of the Emperor and Pahari Rajas. Therefore, he sent back the following message:

Guru Sahib replied,

"I have obtained this from the Sovereign who has made thee Emperor that sent me into the world to do justice. He that commissioned thee also to do justice, but thou hast forgotten His mandate and practice hypocrisy. Wherefore how can I be on good terms with thee who pursues the Hindus with blind hatred? Thou recognizes not that the people belong to God and not to the emperor; and yet thou seekest to destroy their religion".

-Macauliff, Vol V, p. 165

It is noteworthy that Guru Sahib did not agree with Hindu Brahamanical practice, yet he sacrificed his whole family, himself and his Sikhs to protect their right to worship.

Aurangzeb ordered the governors of Delhi, Lahore and Sarhind to send the combined Moghul armies to attack Anandpur Sahib. Macauliffe lists the armies of the following Hindu Pahari Rajas who joined the Mughal forces. Ajmer Chand of Bilaspur, Ghumand Chand of Kangra, Bir Singh of Jaspal, and the Rajas of Kulu, Kointhal, Mandi, Jammu, Noorpur, Chamba, Guler, Siri Nagar (in Garwahl), Bijharwal, Daraub and Dadhwal. The Muslim Ranghars and the Gujars also joined them. The governor of Sarhind Wazir Khan was appointed the supreme commander.

Before the battle engagement, some said that Guru ji's rabble army was weak and not from the warrior class. It would take no time for such a great allied force to decimate them. Some said that the Guru was a miracle worker, and his Khalsa warriors are brave and can never be conquered.

At the end of the first day of Moghul Army and Pahari Raja's attack, 900 of their soldiers lay dead. Guru ji had given the command to his eldest son Ajit Singh to safeguard Kesgarh Sahib, Bhai Nahar Singh and Sher Singh defended the Lohgarh fort. Pyara Daya Singh was to protect the Northern side. Bhai Udhey Singh received a command to defend another part of the city with 500 men. He sent a contingent of 500 Khalsa warriors to hold the Alampur fort. Imagine the mighty Moghal army and thousands soldiers of the combined forces fighting contingents of hundreds of soldiers.

Guru Sahib was directing the operations from a place which was a special target of heavy artillery fire. The Sikhs requested Guru ji to take a less vulnerable place. Guru ji replied that he wore the armor of the Akal Purkh's protection; consequently, no weapon could harm him.

Several small skirmishes took place for the next couple of days, but the attacks were repelled, causing heavy losses. On the third day, the allied army attacked to take the city by storm. The Sikhs brought two of their great guns into action: Baghan (Tigress) and Bijai Gosh (sound of victory). Seeing the devastation caused by these guns, two Moghal generals retreated, and the Pahari Rajas took to flight. As usual, Guru ji thanked Akal Purkh for the victory.

A True Sikh

While the formidable allied armies beleaguered the Sikhs, a Sikh named Kanahiya was serving water to all the injured soldiers, including the enemies. The Sikhs complained to Guru Sahib that they were trying to destroy the enemy soldiers and Bhai Kanahiya was reviving them by giving them water. They called him a traitor. Guru ji summoned Bhai Kanahiya to explain himself. Bhai Kanahiya stood with his hands folded and his head down, and said, " Guru ji, I can't help it because I see your face in every injured soldier's face." Guru ji embraced him and proclaimed that he was a true Sikh. Guru ji gave a first aid kit to Bhai Kanahiya so he could tend to their wounds while he gave them water.

The Siege.

Since the enemy armies failed to conquer the city of Anandpur Sahib, they laid a very tight siege around the fort which continued for eight months. Sometimes the Sikhs would attack the allied positions and seize the food supplies, but they did not last long. Realizing the precarious food situation in the fort, the Pahari Rajas again sent messages. If Guru ji vacated the fort, they promised not to attack Guru ji, they just wanted him to leave Anandpur Sahib. The Sikhs tried to convince Guru ji that this was the safest thing to do. When he did not agree with them, they went to Mata Gujri ji, Guru Sahib's mother. She said that it was time to leave because there was hardly any food left. To demonstrate to the Sikhs, he asked them to create a caravan of wagons filled with all the garbage. He covered the wagons with shining brocades and silks. No sooner did the wagons get out of the fort gates, then the armies pounced on them. The Sikhs understood Guru's reasoning, since many false promises were made. The Sikhs suffered from starvation, and lived by boiling leaves and tree bark. They would not surrender. Their prized horses and Guru ji's gifted elephant died of starvation.

Hundreds of Sikhs sneaked out of the fort after putting in writing that they were no longer his Sikhs. Some reached home and others were killed on the way. Meanwhile, Emperor Aurangzeb sent the following letter:

"I have sworn on the Quoran not to harm thee. If I do, may I not find a place in God's court hereafter! Cease warfare and come to me. If thou desire not to come hither, then go whither soever thou pleasest".

The Emperor's envoy added on his own account,
"O Guru, all who go to the Emperor's court praise thee. On that account the Emperor feeleth certain that an interview with thee will add to his happiness. He hath sworn by Mohammad and called God to witness that he will not harm thee. The hill Rajas have also sworn by the cow and called their idols to witness, that they will allow thee safe conduct.

Bear not in mind anything that had occurred. The attack on thine wagons was not prompted by any Raja. The attackers have been generally punished, and the ringleaders are in prison. No one now, 0 True Guru, dareth do thee harm, wherefore evacuate the fort, at any rate for the present, and come with me to the Emperor. Thou mayest afterwards do what thou pleaseeth."

The Guru on hearing this said,
'You are all liars, and therefore all your empire and your glory shall depart. You all took oaths before this and then perjured yourselves. Your troops, whose business it was to fight, have become robbers, and therefore you shall all be damned.'

(Macauliffe, Vol. V. p 179)

Guru Sahib knew the treachery. Ultimately the remaining Sikhs and Mata Gujri ji prevailed and Guru Sahib decided to leave Anandpur Sahib. By the time Guru Sahib's family and the Sikhs reached Sirsa Nadi (seasonal river), the Moghul forces attacked them. Baba Ajit Singh, the son of Guru Sahib with his jatha, kept the Moghul troops at bay while everybody else crossed the Nadi. A lot of literary works were lost while crossing the flooded Sirsa. Guru Sahib's mother, Mata Gujri ji, took her two younger grand sons Zoravar Singh and Fateh Singh with the Brahmin caretaker Gangu, while Guru Sahib went toward Rupar.

The Battle of Chamkaur Sahib:
Martyrdom of Sahebzadas Ajit Singh and Jhujar Singh

Sri Guru Gobind Singh arrived in Chamkaur Sahib with Panj Payare (Five Beloved Ones), his two sons, Baba Ajit Singh, Baba Jhujar Singh, and a handful of Sikhs. They acquired the residence of two Rajput brothers - a mud brick two-storied Haveli constructed like a small fortress. The older brother Rajput was afraid that Guru Sahib's stay there might invite the wrath of the Moghul Governor of Sarhind. He informed him of Guru Sahib's stay in his Haveli. Soon after, an army of tens of thousands of men beleaguered the fortress and tried to break into it and capture Guru Sahib on December 22, 1704.

Guru Sahib and the Khalsa warriors were well prepared to defend themselves. Their strategy was to cover all sides of the Haveli. Guru Sahib took a position on the second story. Their aim was to shoot down the generals and officers, and not to waste their arrows and bullets on shooting randomly into the troops. General Nahar Khan, the brother of Nawab of Maler Kotla and General Ghairat Khan tried to scale the wall with their troops. They were both shot down by Guru Sahib's arrows. Khwaja Mohammad hid himself against the wall and escaped from being shot down. This discouraged them to take the offensive. It again confirmed their fears, based on their heavy losses in the battles of Anandpur Sahib, that it was dangerous to engage Khalsa warriors in direct fighting.

On the other hand, Guru Sahib took the offensive. He decided to send a jatha of five Sikhs led by a Jathedar (unit commander). Guru Sahib and the Khalsa shot the chosen officers of the Moghul army from the second floor of the Haveli. One of the jathas was led by Guru Sahib's son Baba Ajit Singh, who was only 18 years old. He and his jatha of five Sikhs were killed. Guru Sahib's younger son, Baba Jhujar Singh, requested to be included in the next jatha of six Khalsa warriors, and sacrificed himself with the five other Khalsa warriors. In this way, the Moghul armies were kept at bay during the day. These small Sikh jathas proved the words attributed to Siri Guru Gobind Singh in Punjabi folklore.

Sawa Lakh Se Ek Laraoon
Tabhi Gobind Singh Naam Kahaoon!

I will enable one Khalsa to
Fight one hundred and twenty five thousand;
That would prove the metal of the Khalsa spirit.

Six people in each jatha fought against the army of tens of thousands of Moghul forces. At night, when the forces retired, the Khalsa passed a Gurmata (Guru's resolution). At the time of Amrit ceremony, Sri Guru Gobind Singh ji vested the temporal decision making in the Panj Payare (the Five Beloved Ones). They were the ones who blessed Guru Gobind Singh with the boon of Amrit. They respectfully presented the Gurmata to Sri Guru Gobind Singh ji that requested him to leave the Haveli because he could create more Khalsa. Without him, the Moghuls might succeed in their designs. They requested that two of the five Payare, Bhai Daya Singh, Bhai Dharam Singh and the third Khalsa Man Singh should accompany Guru Sahib. Guru Sahib did not want to leave his beloved Khalsa warriors, but he could not defy the Gurmata. Even now, the Gurmata of the elected Panj Payare from the Sangat prevails. This has been a long tradition in Guru Ghar. The fifth Guru Sri Guru Arjan Dev ji refused to accept the offer of Chandu to marry his daughter to Guru Sahib's son Sri Guru Hargobind ji because the Sangat did not approve of it. Chandu was incensed, and conspired to procure an order for Guru Sahib's execution.

Guru Sahib took the bejeweled plume from his turban and placed it on Bhai Sangat Singh's turban. Then, with three Khalsa warriors, Guru Sahib left the Haveli during the stormy night. He had lost three of the Panj Payare, his two sons and all the Sikhs who were with him. Kirpa Ram, the Brahmin from Kashmir who was the head of the delegation that came to Sri Guru Tegh Bahdur to narrate the suffering of the Brahmins in Kashmir, had become an Amritdhari Khalsa and adopted his name Kirpa Singh. He also gave his life in Chamkaur Sahib battle. The Sikhs who were left in the Haveli, fought unto their death and the Haveli was ultimately destroyed. The Moghuls were happy to see Sangat Singh with Guru Sahib's plume. They mistook him as Guru Gobind Singh, until they discovered that Guru Sahib had escaped and that this was Bhai Sangat Singh's head.

Courage of Guru Sahib's Younger Children

While Guru Sahib was fighting the Moghul army in Chamkaur Sahib, their housekeeper, Gangu Brahmin, was betraying him, to receive a reward from Wazir Khan, the Governor of Sarhind. Guru Sahib's younger sons Baba Fateh Singh and Baba Zorawar Singh, along with their grandmother Mata Gujri ji, were arrested in Morinda. Governor Wazir Khan was happy because it would help him capture Guru Sahib. He ordered them to be brought to Sarhind and imprisoned them in a tower without heat, bedding or food.

Governor Wazir Khan sent a proclamation that Guru Sahib's children would be buried alive in the wall if Guru Sahib did not surrender. At the time, Nawab of Maler Kotla came to visit him. With great pride, Governor Wazir Khan shared his plans of executing Guru Sahib's children and was confident that Guru Sahib would be in his hands after all. To his surprise, Nawab Maler Kotla objected to his plans.

The Nawab reminded him that it is against *Sharah* (the Islamic Law) to execute children and women. Wazir Khan reminded Nawab Sahib that he was pleading for the worst enemy of the Moghul Empire. Wazir Khan reminded him only days before Guru Sahib had killed his brother General Nahar Khan in the battle of Chamkaur.

Nawab of Maler Kotla replied that his brother was killed in a battle, but these small children ages 9 and 7 were not in a battlefield. He declared with a great sad sigh (*Ha Da Nahra*) and grief, if Governor Wazir Khan went through with this most cruel act, history would never forgive him and Sarhind would be in ruins. He walked out of his Darbar chiding the governor for his cruel intentions. Nawab Sahib added that the Guru, who saw his sons dying in front of his eyes in Chamkaur, would never go to him begging for the life of his other two sons. If he ever came, he would bring destruction to Sarhind.

This is just a side comment about the recent past. In 1947, during the partition of India into India and Pakistan (because of the spiritually bankrupt and politically opportunistic leadership of India (1)) there was a total migration of Hindus and Sikhs from Pakistan to India, and Muslims from East Punjab to Pakistan. In addition to a total uprooting of population in West and East Punjab, more than a million people were killed. During this most shameful time in Indian history, the Sikhs remembered the sympathy of Nawab of Maler Kotla toward Guru Sahib's children 300 years ago. Maler Kotla was a Muslim state. No one there was injured or had to leave home. They are still happily living in Indian Punjab.

198

Returning to Governor Wazir Khan's plans, one of his minister's suggested that there was a way that a "snake could be killed without breaking the stick." He advised that they entice these small children to convert to Islam. This would please Emperor Aurangzeb, and the Governor would not be blamed for the death of the children. For Guru Gobind Singh, it would be a humiliation worse than death if his own children embraced Islam. Governor Wazir Khan assigned one of his Hindu ministers Diwan Sucha Mal, to allure the young children to accept Islam. He brought them out of the cold prison tower and entertained them in the palace. He enticed them with all kinds of comforts, sweets and the luxury of princely life in the palace, if they would embrace Islam. They were enraged by any such suggestion. They said that they were the sons of Guru Gobind Singh and had received the same Amrit to be a Khalsa. Nothing could deter them from their spiritual path.

The minister asked them what would they do if the Governor set them free. They said that they would go from village to village and organize the Khalsa army to destroy this cruel regime. He reminded them if they did not accept Islam, they were going to be executed.

When all the efforts failed, Governor Wazir Khan rationalized that these were not innocent children. They were planning a rebellion against the Moghul Empire, therefore, there was a perfect justification for their execution. Since he did not hear from Guru Sahib, he went through with his plans and buried these children alive in a wall.

When the news was conveyed to Mata Gujri ji that her grandchildren Baba Fateh Singh and Baba Zorawar Singh refused to embrace Islam, and embraced death instead, Mataji thanked Waheguru for giving them the courage and strength to live up to their Sikhi spiritual tradition. She left her body and departed for Sach Khand.

12. Travel To Dam Dama Sahib

Sri Guru Gobind Singh Sahib left Chamkaur Sahib and arrived in Machiwara forest. He had already sent his father Guru Tegh Bahadur Sahib to sacrifice himself to preserve the freedom of worship, when he was nine years old. He had sacrificed his four sons and his mother. He had left the comforts of living in well-furnished houses. He was separated from his beloved Khalsa. The Moghul army was pursuing him. After all this, in the solitude of the forests, he wrote the most beautiful message of love to his Beloved Waheguru. He did not complain or question Waheguru's Bhana or pray for rescue from the awful circumstance. In the following verse, he describes his plight in being separated from the Beloved:

mittar pyare nu haal murida da kehna

> Please convey my Beloved Friend
> The plight of It's yearning disciple.
> Without You, rich quilts are agony to me,
> Living in palaces stings me like snakes.
> Decanter is like being impaled on a cross,
> And the cup has an edge like a dagger;
> Separation from you is like
> Being slaughtered by a butcher.
> I prefer lying with my Beloved on a straw mattress,
> To the comforts of Khera, that are like a furnace[1].
>
> -Guru Gobind Singh ji, Dasam Granth

Uch Da Pir (Pir of Village Uch)

There were two Pathan brothers, Nabi Khan and Ghani Khan who were horse traders, who lived in the village Machiwara in the forest. Moghul troops had information that Guru Sahib had gone toward Machiwara. They

---

[1]The last line is a reference from the most adored Punjabi love Ballad of Heer Ranjha. I have translated its symbolic meaning as, "The comforts of Khera are like a furnace. Heer was separated from her beloved Ranjha and was married to the rich chief of Khera.

combed the forest and surrounded the village. The two Pathan brothers planned his escape. They dressed Guru Sahib as a Muslim Faqir from the famous Durgah of village Uch, and sat Guru Sahib on a charpai (cot). Nabi Khan and Ghani Khan put their shoulders in the front. Beloved Daya Singh and Dharam Singh put their shoulders to the rear. They carried him through the village. Bhai Maan Singh did the Chaur Sewa (fanning him in respect). When they came face to face with the Moghul army, they replied to questioning that they were carrying Uch Da Pir (Pir of Village Uch). Thus they helped Guru ji escape.

Guru Da Bhana (Gods's Will)

From Machiwara, Guru Sahib went toward Beas River. His uncle Kaul Rai Sodhi, lived in a nearby village. Uncle Kaul Rai had heard the stories of atrocities and the loss of Guru Sahib's four sons and his mother, and the stories of the sacrifices of Guru Sahib's beloved Sikhs. He was filled with grief, and with tears in his eyes he expressed his sorrow and wondered about how Guru Sahib could bear such losses. Guru Sahib asked Beloved Daya Singh to draw four lines on the ground. Then he asked him to erase them. He asked him again to draw four lines and asked him to erase them. Guru Sahib repeated this four times. In the end, Guru Sahib asked Beloved Daya Singh if he experienced any change in his feelings while he drew the lines and erased them. Beloved Daya Singh answered, he did not experience any change in his feelings, he was just carrying out the orders of his Guru.

Guru Sahib explained that we come into this world according to Waheguru's Hukam (Orders). We return to him according to his Hukam. According to His Hukam, we receive the gifts, we enjoy them and they are taken away "Like Bhai Daya Singh ji we just obey orders of Waheguru." They were his gifts and he has taken them back.

Zafarnama (The Epistle of Victory)

You may recall that Emperor Auragzeb wrote two letters to Sri Guru Gobind Singh ji before Guru Sahib left Anandpur Sahib. He received the third letter on his way to Sabo Ki Talwandi at Dina near the village Kangar. There he wrote his famous Zafarnama in Farsi poetry, a reply to Aurangzeb. It has three parts. The first part is an invocation to God describing the true nature of Allah and his attributes, such as,

"— Perfect in beauty. Merciful, Master of knowledge, Support of the unhappy. Searcher of hearts. Author of revelation, Appreciator of wisdom. Lord of Intelligence, Decipher of secrets. Omnipresent God, Thou resolves its difficulties. Thou art its great organizer." (11)

The second part describes the atrocities Emperor Aurangzeb heaped upon the non-Muslim subjects entrusted to him by God. Guru Sahib chided Aurangzeb for not knowing anything about Prophet Muhammad.

> Thou knoweth not God, believest not in Muhammad.
> He who hath regard for his religion
> Never swerved from his promise.
> Thou hast no idea of what an oath on Quoran is
> And canst have no belief in Divine Providence". (11)

Guru Sahib talked about his deceit, treachery and broken promises. Guru Sahib described the battle of Chamkaur Sahib and the murder of his young children in Sarhind. He gave a challenge,

> "What though my four sons have been killed,
> the coiled cobra still remains." (11)

Guru Sahib invited the Emperor,

"If thou come to the village of Kangar, we shall have an interview. Thou shalt not run the slightest danger on the way, for the whole tribe of Brars is under my influence. Come to me so that we may speak to each other And that I may utter kind words to thee".

In the third part of Zafarnama, Guru Sahib again discussed God and how Aurangzeb had totally forsaken God in every respect.

" I do not deem thou knowest God, Since thou hast done acts of oppression Thou art proud of thy army and wealth. I repose my trust and confidence in the King of Kings, When God is a friend, millions of enemies can not do any harm".

Guru Sahib entrusted Beloved Bhai Daya Singh and Beloved Bhai Dharam Singh to deliver the letter to Emperor Aurangzeb. Aurangzeb was very interested in meeting Guru Sahib, but he died before he had the chance to visit him.

Muktsar (The Pool of Salvation)

During the eight-month siege at the Anandpur Sahib Fort, forty Sikhs from Majha (Lahore and Amritsar Districts) had given in writing a declaration to Sri Guru Gobind Singh Sahib that he was not their Guru and they were not his Sikhs. When the Sikhs returned home, their wives disapproved of their desertion of the Guru. They shamed the Sikhs by saying that they should wear Churian (glass bangles) on their arms and give their weapons to them so that they could fight instead. The Sikhs realized their blunder, and decided to return to Guru Sahib and ask for his forgiveness. They were led by Bhai Mahan Singh of Sursingh and Mata (Mother) Bhago ji of Jhabal.

At that time, Guru Sahib was headed toward Sabo Ki Talwandi, which later came to be known as Dam Dama Sahib because it was where Guru Sahib had decided to rest. The Moghul army of Governor Wazir Khan of Sirhand wanted to attack Guru Sahib on the way, and finish him and his Khalsa for good.

They decided to go to Khidrana, where there was a pool of water in the desert. The forty Sikhs who had deserted Guru Sahib, decided to join Guru Sahib at Khidrana to fight back the Moghul army. The Moghul army was disappointed to find the Khidrana pool of water dry. The small number of Sikhs spread sheets of cloth on the great number of bushes to make it look like a vast encampment of Sikhs. They attacked the Moghul army on May 8, 1705, one of the hottest months in Punjab. By that time, Guru Sahib had also arrived. He took a position at a small hill, and continued a shower of his arrows. The Moghul army was defeated and fled; most of the forty Sikhs lay dead. Guru Sahib went to each of them, and showered his love and blessings.

When he came to Bhai Mahan Singh, he was wounded but still alive. Guru Sahib cleaned his face, gave him water and asked him what he wanted as a reward for his bravery. Bhai Mahan Singh said that he wanted Guru Sahib to tear up the paper on which he and his forty companions had declared that they were not his Sikhs. Guru Sahib complied with his wishes and blessed him before he breathed his last. He also blessed the place and the pool as a place of salvation to commemorate the martyrdom of the forty brave Sikhs. It is called Mukatsar, The pool of emancipation.

Mata Bhago was still alive and recovered from her wounds. She stayed with Guru Sahib until he departed for Sach Khand in 1708 at Hazur Sahib.

The Days At Dam Dama Sahib
Muktsar was the last battle. After Guru Sahib arrived at Dam Dama Sahib, he got busy imparting spiritual instructions to people who came to see him from far and wide. He sent a delegation of 25 Sikhs to bring the Adi Granth from his cousin Dhirmal. He refused to part with Adi Granth and

he challenged: if Gobind Singh is truly a Guru, then why doesn't he create his own? Why did he need to ask for the one he had? The Sikhs reported back to Sri Guru Gobind Sahib what Dhirmal said.

If Guru Sahib wanted, he could have sent his Khalsa to forcibly recover the Adi Granth from Dhirmal family. Instead, he dictated 1430 pages of Sri Guru Granth Sahib, with all the complicated editing details that Sri Guru Arjan Dev ji had used in compiling the Adi Granth. It included identifying each verse with the author, the Raag in which it should be sung, and the number and poetical form of the verse and the punctuation. This was accomplished in the exact order as the Adi Granth. Guru Sahib added the Sloaks of Sri Guru Tegh Bahadur Sahib to it. Bhai Mani Singh was the transcriber and Baba Deep Singh was his assistant. The Adi Granth does not separate each word. It is written in the old Sanskrit style in which the words are not separated.

Mata Sundri ji and Mata Sahib Kaur joined him from Delhi. Mata Sundri ji asked him about the loss of her four sons. He uttered the following famous words, pointing to the Khalsa:

chaar mooey to kia hooa jab jeevat kaee hazaar

"What if four have died when thousands are still alive"?

13. Helping Emperor Bahadur Shah

Emperor Auangzeb died in February 1707. At that time, his eldest son Bahadur Shah, was going toward Afghanistan. The younger son, Muhammad Azim, was in Dakhan with the emperor and declared himself as the emperor. He took over the treasury and command of the army. As the eldest son, Bahadur Shah wanted to regain his throne, but he was no match for Muhammad Azim's army. He knew the proven power of the

Khalsa against the allied armies of Moghul governors of Sirhand and Lahore, and the armies of the Pahari Rajas. Bhai Nand Lal was Bahadur Shah's teacher before he escaped from his father Emperor Aurangzeb's design to convert him to Islam. He had been a Sikh of Guru Gobind Singh and the most distinguished poet among the scholars and poets of Guru Sahib's Darbar in Anandpur Sahib. Bahadur Shah approached Bhai Nand Lal to go to Sri Guru Gobind Singh ji for help.

It is noteworthy that the father of Bahadur Shah executed Guru Sahib's father Sri Guru Tegh Bahadur Sahib. Guru Sahib fought continuously against Moghul armies who tried to annihilate all the Sikhs and their Guru. He had lost his four sons, his mother, his father and hundreds of his beloved Khalsa warriors, fighting against the armies of the Moghuls. In spite of all that, when Bhai Nand Lal brought the request from Bahadur Shah, Guru Gobind Singh ji decided to help him to his rightful claim to the throne. Guru Sahib sent the Khalsa warriors under the command of Bhai Dharam Singh. After Bahadur Shah regained his throne, he invited Guru Sahib to his coronation. Emperor Bahadur Shah presented Guru Sahib the sword, which the Imam of Mecca had presented to Aurangzeb when he went for Haj.

Guru Gobind Singh and Bahadur Shah remained friends ever since.

14. Sri Hazur Sahib

Sri Guru Gobind Singh Sahib traveled with emperor Bahadur Shah and spent time discussing religion and poetry. Then he parted company with Bahadur Shah and traveled south to Dakhan to settle in a small place on the banks of Godavri in Hydrabad. Now it is called Abchal Nagar Hazur Sahib. He continued his spiritual instructions and had morning and evening Sangat Darbar.

Banda Singh Bahadur.

There lived a Bairagi Madho Das in the vicinity of Hazur Sahib, formerly a great hunter and a warrior. Once, he shot a pregnant dear with his arrow. He was so touched by this event that he renounced the world and became a Bairagi (ascetic). Guru Sahib went to his Ashram, sat on his couch and waited for him. When Bairagi Madho Das returned and saw a stranger sitting in his exalted seat, he became very incensed and tried to hurt Guru Sahib with his occult and psychic powers, but nothing could affect Guru Sahib. Ultimately, he realized that he was in divine presence. He became Guru Sahib's Sikh. It appears that Guru Sahib had known about him and sought him to perform a unique service to Guru Sahib. He became an Amridhari Khalsa. When he surrendered to Guru Sahib, he said "I am your Banda," a devotee. Guru Sahib named him Banda Singh. "Bahadur" means brave. Because of his bravery when he came to Punjab, he is known as Banda Singh Bahadur.

Guru Sahib chose Banda Singh Bahadur to go to Punjab and uproot the oppressive rule of Governor Wazir Khan. Guru Sahib gave him five of his arrows and five Sikhs to accompany him. He sent Hukam Namas (orders) to all the Sikhs to join Banda Singh under his command to uproot the oppressive regime of Governor of Sirhand.

On the other hand, after the Govenor of Sirhand found out about the alliance between Guru Sahib and Emperor Bahadur Shah, he feared for his life and sent two of his trusted Pathans to assassinate Guru Sahib. They went to Hazur Sahib and joined the Sangat. People from different faiths always joined the Sangat. No suspicions were raised. One evening, they found an opportune time to assassinate the Guru while Guru Sahib was resting in bed. He was stabbed in his belly by one of the assassins. Guru Sahib held the Pathan with one hand, pulled out the dagger from his belly, and finished the assassin with his own dagger. The Sikhs killed the Pathan's accomplice.

Guru Sahib's wound was well attended to and healing adequately. One day, he received a gift of a bow and arrow. When he tried it out, his wound reopened and blood started gushing out. Guru Sahib knew that his time had come to depart to Sach Khand. His wound was stitched and bandaged. Guru Sahib bathed himself, and dressed himself in his regalia. According to the custom of passing on Baba Nanak's Light to the next Guru, Sri Guru Gobind Singh ji took a coconut and five paise (pennies) as an offering before Sri guru Granth Sahib and said,

aagiya bhaee akaal ki tabi chalao panth

> According to the command of Akal Purkh
> I started the Panth.
> All Sikhs are ordered
> To accept Guru The Granth
> Believe Guru Granth ji
> As the manifest body of the Gurus
> Who so ever wants to meet the Beloved
> Will find Him in the Shabad.
> -Giani Gian Singh, Panth Prakash - P.353

Guru Gobind Singh ji departed for Sachkhand in October 1708. He had already made Khalsa in his true image. The Sikhs receive spiritual guidance from Sri Guru Granth Sahib. For worldly, day-to-day affairs of the Panth, the Sangat is supreme that acts through the elected *Prabhandak* Committees (Managment Committees) of local Gurdwaras and the Shiromani Gurdawara Prabhandhak committee (S.G.P.C.) manages the historical Sikh Gurdwaras. Unfortunately, S.G.P.C. is not elected in a democratic (one person one vote) way. Some of the local Gurdwaras, in the United States, the Prabhandhak Committee members, are also not elected directly by the Sangat. There are very complicated reasons for doing so, which require a detailed analysis; a separate subject in itself. Suffice it to say that it is unfortunate that at present, the Sangat is not given the same respect as is given by the Gurus. The Haumain based elitist mentality has crept in. In some Gurdwaras, the Prabhadak Committee is selected by so called "Amritdhari Sikhs," who maintain the Khalsa appearance. In others, the "sophisticated" Sikhs who are rich and educated maintain the control of the Gurdwaras. The Haumain King prevails instead of Amrit Naam.

Guru Sangat had made Khalsa ("Guru Sangat Keeni Khalsa"). Unless there is a vibrant Gursangat, the Khalsa Panth has no foundation to stand on. To maintain and nurture Sat Sangat by imparting Gurbani spiritual practice to our coming generations and seek that guidance for ourselves, is the only way to maintain Sikh spiritual consciousness and preserve Khalsa as Akal Purkh's army and not a sectarian religious organization that fights for material and political gains.

The Summary Contrast of the Consciousness, the loving devotion to Naam that Motivated Sri Guru Gobind Singh ji, The Khalsa, VS Aurangzeb, The Emperor, motivated by Haumain.

Sri Guru Gobind Singh ji, The Khalsa

1. Believed in one God

2. Believed that Baba Nanak's house and Emperor Babar's house received their authority from Waheguru, the Creator. Baba Nanak for spiritual guidance and Babar to be the emperor.

3. The creator is called by different names, yet It is One. We are all It's children. They should be served and nurtured.

4. Lived in spiritual consciousness while being a householder and a selfless warrior to protect those who could not protect themselves.

5. a) He was aware of the destructive power of Haumain attachment which distracts you from Waheguru consciousness.

   b) He was detached from Haumain and was totally guided by Waheguru consciousness.

Aurangzeb, The Emperor

1. Believed in one God.

2. Believed in a sectarian God who gave only Muslims the Authority to rule. To please Allah, he had to convert everyone else to Islam by persuasion or force; especially those who were outstanding, such as Bhai Nand Lal.

3. Allah is the only right name; those who do not believe in Allah are infidels and should be converted, even by force, or tortured to death.

4. Lived in sectarian religious consciousness. Was also a householder, great warrior, but a conqueror.

5. a) He had no awareness of the Haumain's destructive power and was distracted from Allah consciousness. His Haumain made him a religious fanatic.

   b) He was attached to Haumain consciousness. He was totally guided by it, including his religious fervor.

c) All of us are children of Waheguru, therefore, he ushered in equality and non-sectarian, no caste or class society.

c) He considered Muslims the chosen ones of Allah. Considered others infidels and discriminated against non-Muslims. Considered Muslims the superior race.

d) He fought and sacrificed his father, mother and four sons to protect the poor, the vulnerable and the oppressed.

d) He fought to satisfy his Haumain. To acquire his personal power, he killed his three brothers and imprisoned his father.

e) During the battles all spiritually awakened persons, the Muslim Pirs and Faqirs and Hindu Sadhus fought on his side to protect the oppressed and victims of unjust and cruel rulers.

e) During the battles, all the Haumain attached persons who were motivated by Haumain and personal power, such as Hindu Pahari Rajas, and Muslim Nawabs, fought on Aurangzeb's side.

f) He was always victorious because Aurangzeb could never subjugate or destroy his spirit and wrote the Epistle of Victory, Zafarnama, after all the suffering.

f) He was always frustrated, because he never could subjugate Guru Gobind Singh. After receiving Zafarnama, the Epistle of Victory, he realized how his Haumain-based fanatic religious fervor was non-Muslim consciousness which did not please Allah, the Creator of us all and not just Muslims, Christians, Hindus, or Jews etc. He longed to meet Guru Gobind Singh before he died.

6. Guru Gobind Singh was fearless (Nirbhao), spiritually, totally merged with the eternal (Akal), therefore life and death, the transitory states had no meaning, He

6. He was not merged with the Eternal. He was fearful that he might lose his temporal power. He saw even his own brothers and father as enemies.

was Eternal. The Khalsa consciousness makes one eternal; He was Nirver (no emimity) the sixth Guru saved Jahangir's life, who murdered his father. Guru Gobind Singh saved Bahadur Shah's throne, whose father Aurangzeb murdered Guru Sahib's father Guru Tegh Bahadur.

This Divine play as stated before has been staged in different parts of the world throughout history; only the names and places were different. Christ was persecuted by the power elite of Romans and Pharasies instead of Brahmins, Moghuls and Pahari Rajas in India. Hazrat Mohammad Sahib was persecuted by the power elite of Mecca.

Implications for Peace and Harmony

This divine play has implications for our personal life, and peace and harmony on earth.

1. We can evaluate ourselves, how far we live in Haumain consciousness, attachment to our body and motivated by its extensions of greed, lust, anger and personal pride.

2. How much we live in spiritual consciousness and how much in Haumain based sectarian religious consciousness.

3. How much time and effort do we spend nurturing our love for the divine and merge with the divine? Perceive Divine in everything and everyone and selflessly serve the Divine and Its Creation. How much time and effort do we spend in fueling the fire of our Haumain?

4. To be a spiritual warrior, one does not have to be an army soldier. First, one has to fight to keep detached from Haumain and its extension, Lust, Anger, Greed, and Pride, and merge with the Divine.

The person who fights with his Haumain self
is the greatest warrior.
The one who has recognized his Self
is eternally merged with the Divine.

-SGGS - P. 1089

5. How far we live in divine consciousness and accept the Divine will, Bhana, Raza or God's will.

6. To what extent we love and serve the Divine. Whatever role is given to us by the Divine, we try to live that role in Divine consciousness and serve the Divine and Its Creation selflessly. Meditate on Naam, make an honest living, share with the needy, and protect the vulnerable and oppressed against the oppression and injustice by the people motivated by Haumain consciousness.

If I am a poor laborer, I still live in Divine consciousness. If I am a politician member of the ruling class, I should serve Creator's people. If I am a technocrat, computer software engineer, I have been given more opportunity for service. If I am in a helping profession, I have been given even a greater opportunity to serve the Divine. If I am a clergy, stay connected with the One Divine and the spiritual consciousness. Do not get over powered by Haumain, and perperuate a sectarian religion. All "Spiritually Awake" Avtars, Prophets, Bhagats, and Pir, Faqirs and Saints had the same experience; Love is the path to divine. God is Love! No one ever said God is Hatred! Hatred is a disease. Instead of rationalizing it, let us seek treatment. The spiritually enlightened beings tried to impress upon the ruling class that loving and nurturing God's children pleases God. They tried to uplift the poor and oppressed. Moses liberated the Jews from the Pharoh's oppression. Christ liberated the Jews from the oppression of the Pharisees and Romans. His disciples were common suffering humanity, not the money-lenders and the ruling class. He said, "The meek shall inherit the earth". Hazrat Muhamand Sahib also came to liberate people from superstition and fighting among different tribes. He preached love of God and equality. Guru Nanak and Guru Gobind Singh also came to liberate humanity from Haumain bondage that creates oppression and exploitation of human beings by other human beings.

Unfortunately, the name of the spiritual beings get used by the Haumain motivated power elite. After Romans became Christians, they did not adopt a loving non-violent Christ consciousness; instead the "Christians" used Christ to create oppression and misery in this world. The same is true of most religions. They use the spiritual being's name to accomplish their Haumain motivated goals. The latest example is the Sikhs. In the name of Guru Nanak, Guru Gobind Singh they fight for sectarian political goals, instead of serving humanity with love and self sacrifice.

If you are a part of the power elite: academia, clergy, business, media people, or political ruling class, you have the greatest opportunity and responsibility to serve the Divine and Its creation. Until now, all of our institutions are based on Haumain attachment and motivated by lust, greed, power, pride and anger. We resort to violence to achieve our Haumain goals.

pariah moorakh akhieh

> "An educated person be called a fool
> who has greed, attachment and pride."
>
> -Asa Di Var

If these institutions are based on Divine love and the motivation to serve humanity, there can be peace, harmony and prosperity for all. There are great hopeful signs. There are literally hundreds of grass root organizations working toward peace, preserving the environment, economic justice, and United Religions Initiative started by Episcopalian Bishop Bill Swing, human rights organizations and political reform initiatives nationally, internationally, and through the United Nations.

If we do not recognize the impact of Haumain consciousness and replace it with Divine consciousness, all our efforts will come to naught. History tells us that all spiritual and political revolutions were started by grassroots movements with humanistic intentions. As soon as the movements succeeded, the new leadership behaved in the same despotic and exploitive way.

Every village, town and city in this world has a Church, Mosque, Temple or a Gurdwara. Can you imagine what joy, peace and harmony could prevail on the planet if the Ministers, Priests, Mullas, Brahmins, Monks and Bhai jis engaged in providing spiritual guidance and instructions, instead of propagating Haumain based sectarian religious practices. If all their followers truly began to live in spiritual consciousness, loving devotion to our Creator and its Creation, what an eternal joy would pervade in this universe!

VII. Selected Bibliography

1. Azad, Maulana Abul Kalam,(1960)India Wins Freedom. Longman Green and Co., New York, London Toronto.
2. Chahal, Pritam Singh, Siri Guru Granth Sahib in Punjabi with English translation printed by Mrs. Manuj Jesbir Singh at Crescent Printing Works,P-14, Connaught Circus New Delhi- 110001, India
3. Danaher, Kevin (1994), 50 Years Is Enough: The Case Against The World Bank And The International Monetary Fund -South End Press M.A.
4. Gupta, Hari Ram, (1995 ed.) History of The Sikhs, Vol. IV. The Sikh Commonwealth or Rise and Fall of Sikh Misls. Munshi Ram Manohar Lal Publishes Pvt. Ltd. 54 Rani Jhansi Road, New Delhi 110055
5. Gupta, Hari Ram (1991, First Edition), History of the Sikhs Vol.V The Sikh Lion of Lahore (Mahraja Ranjit Singh (1799-1839). Munshi Ram Manohar Lal Publishers Private Ltd. 54 Rani Jhansi Raod, New Delhi 10055.
6. Gurbani Researcher(1998). International Institute of Gurmat Studies. Justin, California. Phone: 714, 669-1770. It is one CD Rom Disc containing Sri Guru Granth Sahib in Punjabi, English translation and Punjabi Font.
7. Gurdas, Bhai (1994), Varan Gian Ratnavali, Shiromani Prabhandhak Committee, Amritsar
8. Kartin, David C. (1995), When Corporations Rule the World, Co-Published by Kunarian Press, and Barret-Kohler Publishers Inc. 155 Montgomery St. San Francisco.
9. Kohli, Surinder Singh, (1996) Dictionary of Guru Granth Sahib. Singh Brothers Mai Sewan Bazar, Amritsar.
10. Mann, Gurninder Singh,(2001) The Making of Sikh Scriptures, Oxford University Press, New York.
11. Macauliffe, Max Arthur,(1978) The Sikh Religion (I to VI vols.). S.Chand and Company Ltd. Ram Nagar, New Delhi-110 055.

12. Padam, Piara Singh (1969 Punjabi), Guru Granth Veechaar kosh, Punjabi University, Patiala, Punjab, India.

13. Padam, Piara Singh (ed) (1997), Pracheen Sau Sakhi by Bhai Sahib Singh, Singh Brothers, Amritsar.

14. Sikh Rahit Maryada (1979), Shiromani Gurdwara Prabhadhak Committee, Amritsar

15. Singh, Baba Santa (2000), Sri Sarabh Loh Granth Sabib ji Steek, Vol. 2, Baba Budha Dal, Patiala.

16. Singh, Bhai Sahib (1961), Sri Guru Granth Sahib, Punjabi Translation, Raj Publishers, Jullundar, Punjab, India.

17. Singh, Bhai Veer Singh (1986 Punjabi),Puratan Janam Sakhi Sri Guru Nanak Dev ji, Khalsa Samachar, Amritsar.

18. Singh, Gian (1987), Panth Prakash, Bhasha Vibhag, Patiala

19. Singh, Gopal, (1978), Sri Guru Granth Sahib English Translation, World Sikh University Press, Chandigarh, Punjab,India

20. Singh, Mohinder, (1978), The Akali Movement, The National Institute of Panjabi Studies, New Delhi.

21. Singh, Narain, Punabi Translation of Sri Dasam Granth Sahib ji by Sri Guru Gobind Singh ji, Bhai Chatar Singh Jeevan Singh, Bazar Mai Sevan, Amritsar.

22. Singh, R. K. Janmeja (2001), A Tragic Wake Up Call, The Hume Center, Concord, California

23. Singh, R.K. Janmeja (1975) Beyond Camelot, A Conceptual Model of Organizational Dynamics, The Hume Center, Concord, California

24. Singh, Santokh (1992) Nitnaym Banees – Daily Sikh Prayers, Sikh Resource Center, Princeton, Ontario, Canada.

25. Singh, Trilochan; Singh, Jodh; Singh, Kapur; Singh, Bawa Harkrishan; Singh, Khushwant (1960), The Sacred Writings of The Sikhs, UNESCO Collection of Representative Works. Indian Series, Printed In Great Britain by Unwin Brothers London.

GLOSSARY

A

Akal: Beyond Time – eternal. This is one of the attributes of the Creator.

Amrit: Nector of eternity. Among the Sikhs it holds a great importance and is used in the following ways:
1. Amrit Naam Nidhan Hai
   The boon of eternity (Amirt) is Naam.
2. The Sikh initiation into Khalsa ceremony is called Amrit Sanchar.
3. Amrit dhari is the one who has been initiated as Khalsa by partaking Amrit and thus becomes, eternal. Meditating on Naam and Gurbani Simran are necessary to alleviate Haumain and merge with the Eternal and become Eternal.

B

Bhagat: Devotee, saint

Bhat: Bard

Bhog: The end. Among Sikhs it is used in the following ways:
1. Bhog ceremony at the completion of Sri Guru Granth Sahib reading.
2. Bhog of Deevan (End of Sikh religious ceremony or service).

D

Dharamsaal: A place of worship also in Punjabi villages there is a free "inn" for travelers through the village or for other village functions, such as wedding parties.

Deevan: A religious celebration where people recite Sikh poetry, Gurbani Kirtan or lectures on Sikhi, Gurus' lives, Sikh history or Sikh political affairs.

Durbar: Traditionally it is used for royal court. Since the Creator is king of kings the Sikhs call Golden Temple Darbar Sahib or Harmandir Sahib. A big Sikh congregation is also called Darbar, such as Kavi Darbar (poetical symposium).

G
Guru: Enlightener. Sikhs also called the Creator Guru.

Guru Ghar: The house of the Guru.

Gurbani: Guru's word. Verses written by the Gurus.

Gurmantar: Guru's word to meditate on .
For Sikhs Waheguru is Gurmantar.

Granthi: Who interprets Gurbani and Sri Guru Granth Sahib.

Gurdwara: The threshold of the Guru. The Sikh place of worship is called Gurdwara.

H
Haumain: It literally means "I AM". It is the individual consciousness that experiences one's sojourn in a given body through this world. It could be close to little "me" or ego personality.

Hankar: Pride

I
Ik Onkar: The attribute of the Creator: One Creator that manifests itself in the Creation.

J
Ji: A word at the end of a name signifying affectionate regards and respect, such as, Sri Guru Nanak Dev ji

K

Karta: Creator

Kaam: Lust

Karma: deeds. In Sikh scriptures, it is Haumain that experiences Karma, our deeds. Reduced attachment to Haumain also reduces the impact of Karma.

Khalsa: The pure one. A person who has partaken Amrit and cleanses himself /herself with Naam Simran and Gurbani recitation is striving toward becoming a Khalsa.

Kirt: Work toward earning a living.

Kirtan: Singing of Gurbani.

L

Lavan: Circumambulation around Sri Guru Granth Sahib during the Sikh wedding ceremony. Hindus circle around the sacred fire.

Lobh: Greed

M

Moh: Attachment

N

Naam: Literally means name. In Sikh scriptures it is used for the identity of the Creator who is transcendental as well as manifests Itself in Its Creation. Each of us has Naam ingrained in our consciousness. The purpose of the Sikh Spiritual practice is to alleviate Haumin (I Am) and realize the cosmic divine Naam consciousness to guide our actions in this world.

Nirver: Without enmity.

P

Panth: A religious community or organization such as, Khalsa Panth.

Pangat: Sitting together to receive Langar (the blessed food in a Gurdwara).

Purkh: The Creative Force or Energy. Also Man.

S

Sadh: Saint; one who has relinquished his/her Haumain.

Sadh Sangat: Sangat means companionship.
Companionship of the saints. Sikh congregation is called Sadh Sangat.

Sahib: Master. It is also used as a word of respect for elders.

Sant: Saint

Sant Sipahi: Spiritual warrior.

Sehaj: A state of spiritual equanimity

Sewa: Selfless service.

Shabad: Word. The verses written by Sikh Gurus.

Sikh: A disciple, learner or a seeker.
Sipahi: Soldier

Sri Guru Granth Sahib: The holy book of the Sikhs. The Sikhs consider it as their eternal Guru.

V

Vaar: Ballad

Vairag: Longing for the Beloved.

Vand Chhkna: To share with the needy what one has for one's own use.

W

Waheguru: The wondrous Creator. It is an exclamation experiencing the
beauty and mysteries of this universe. For Sikhs it is Gurmantar.
You meditate on this experience and remember it all the time.
The Sikhs begin everything by first saying Waheguru even when
they start their car.

Appendix -I
Feedback Questionnaire

If you answer the following questionnaire and mail it to me or e-mail at meji@pavior.com along with your corrections and comments, I will be very thankful. Your feedback will help my own development and will help create a dialogue and fellowship.

I. Name:_____

Address:_____

Phone _____   Fax _____

E-mail _____

Your Spiritual Path or Religion:_____

II: Content :

(1) Please list your questions about the concepts or ideas, which were not clear to you.

(2) List your ideas or concepts that are contrary to those presented in this book.

(a) If you are not a Sikh, write down the concepts or stories in your spiritual practice that are similar to presented in this book.

(b). If you are not a Sikh, write down the concepts or stories in your spiritual practice, that are contrary to those presented in this manuscript.

III. Overall Evaluation:

1. What did you find in this book, that was new or useful to you?

2. What parts you think should be changed or excluded.

3. What parts of the book were of most interest to you?

4. Any additional comments or suggestions.

Appendix-II

Ik Onkar
Peace Foundation

P.O. Box 10896 • Pleasanton, CA 94588

IK ONKAR PEACE FOUNDATION
Articles of Incorporation
Preamble

Ik Onkar means there is one Divine Creator who manifests It self in Its Creation. This implies that the essence of all beings is the same Divine. Every one and every thing in this universe is sacred. The divine is both immanent and transcendental. There is a Divine Order that governs the creation,

> "Everything is in Divine Order there is nothing outside of it.
> If one understands this then one
> does not make Haumain based claims."
>
> -Guru Nanak Dev ji

You and I are in essence the same. What keeps us apart is my Haumain i.e., "I am" consciousness. Attachment to Haumain is the cause of all suffering. The second type of consciousness is Naam or Divine consciousness. The purpose of a spiritual journey is to realize the Divine within our selves, live in this cosmic or divine consciousness and reduce the Haumain consciousness. Perceiving divine in everything alleviates duality.

> The sense of enmity and estrangement is vanished
> Since I have been in the company of saints. (Reflective pause)

Foe and stranger there is none;
I am at peace with everyone
Whatever the Beloved commands I accept with pleasure;
This is the wisdom I received from the saints.
Waheguru resides in every body
Beholding it in every one Nanak is in a state of bliss.

-Guru Arjan Dev ji

Mission

The mission of the Ik Onkar Peace Foundation is to promote Divine Consciousness through spiritual practice, workshops, conferences, seminars and publications. To reduce greed and promote economic and social justice, preserve the planetary beauty and resources, work toward peace within and in relationship to each other and harmony in the world, promote peaceful conflict resolution and prevent war.

Ik Onkar Peace Foundation is an inter-faith tax exempt corporation. It is also a cooperation circle of United Religions Initiative (U.R.I.)

Appendix-III

Ik Onkar
੧ੴ *Peace Foundation*

P.O. Box 10896 • Pleasanton, CA 94588

PEACE RESOLUTION

In awareness of the rising tide of conflicts on the planet, and the increase in poverty, injustice and suffering, the Ik Onkar Peace Foundation offers the following resolution in support of authentic, everlasting Peace:

BE IT RESOLVED, that the Ik Onkar Peace Foundation expresses its support for the Principle that the divine spirit is within each of us, manifests itself in Love and Truth, and is found through the opening of the heart;

BE IT FURTHER RESOLVED, that the way to Peace begins, but does not end with the individual and extends to the family, the community and the Planet, and is a Journey of inspiration and action that all are called to;

BE IT FURTHER RESOLVED, that Peace comes with the open hearted recognition that all life is sacred, that the Divine Presence can be found through many paths, and that God and the Divine Presence can neither be owned nor expressed in a single way or by a single group, but to be fully realized and expressed requires the participation of all;

THEREFORE, the Ik Onkar Peace Foundation, through its activities and the actions of its members, acknowledges the need to end war, to end the use of violence as a means of resolving conflict, to end the use of oppression as a means of establishing dominance, and the propagation of a single ideology of economics or religion as the only true path to Peace. It commits to work through the individual and the community to bring Peace through Dialogue, Communication, Meditation, use of conflict resolution technology and Connection to the Divine Presence Bring this resolution to other groups for review, refinement, and endorsement.

Prepared by Ralph Wolff and unanimously adopted by the Ik Onkar Peace Foundation Board of Trustees on May 17, 2003

Reviewed and endorsed by:

Organization	Represented by
Address	Phone/fax
Email	Date

Comments/Recommendations for Improvement:

Please return the completed resolution with your comments to Ik Onkar Peace Foundation by mail, or e-mail: meji@pavior.com

Meji Singh, Ph.D. Since 1991 he has been a Visiting Professor/Lecturer in Psychology at the University of California, Berkeley. He is the President Emeritus and Chief Psychologist at Portia Bell Hume Behavioral Health and Training Center, Concord, California. He was one of the founders (1964) of the Sikh Center of San Francisco Bay Area, El Sobrante Gurdwara. Since 1990 he has been teaching Gurbani (Sikh Scriptures) to children and youth at the Gurdwara. He was the Founding Trustee and Secretary of the Sikn Foundation of North America, Redwood city, California (1966-74). Singh is a member of the Board of Directors of Inter-Faith Center at the Presidio in San Francisco. He is president of the Ik Onkar Peace Foundation. He was the Dean of the Rosebridge Graduate School of Integrative Psychology for ten years and the Assistant Director of The Center For Training In Community Psychiatry and Mental Health Administration at Berkeley for fourteen years. For 2 years he worked in a State Hospital and for 16 years in Community Mental Health Programs.

On the basis of his experience as a clinical psychologist and an organizational consultant, along with his study of Sikh scriptures, he has presented a Paradigm for Peace and Harmony. So far the evolution of human civilization is dominated by greed, power and violence. Now we have sufficient peaceful conflict resolution technology available to evolve our civilization and preserve the planet based on a paradigm of love, care and service of our fellow human beings.